The Blueprint for

2 AMERICAS

*Lets Make America.
Godly Again

Linda*

LINDA NELSON

www.2americas.net

ISBN 978-1-0980-9869-8 (paperback)
ISBN 978-1-0980-9870-4 (digital)

Christian Faith Publishing, Inc.
832 Park Avenue
Meadville, PA 16335
www.christianfaithpublishing.com

Printed in the United States of America

DEDICATION

One of God's gifts that most perfectly reflects His love for me is the gift of companionship. My life has been blessed by the companionship of a husband whose gifts, talents, kindness, humor, and intelligence surpasses anyone else I have ever had the privilege to know.

While I had a passion to get the information in this little book into the public conversation, my precious husband, Robert, liberally lavished his support, his editing skills, and his encouragement upon me so that I could complete the project. I consider myself the richest woman on earth to have shared my life with such a stunning person, and I'm privileged to dedicate this book to Robert, the love of my life who correctly says that we must make America godly again!

SPECIAL THANKS

Illustrations by Jacob H. Holt

Information and Marketing Services by Michael D. Erickson LLC

CONTENTS

Abraham Lincoln in his acceptance speech for the nomination for United States Senator in Springfield, Illinois on June 16, 1858 said in part:

> "I believe this government cannot endure
> permanently half slave and half free.
> I do not expect the Union to be dissolved —
> I do not expect the house to fall —
> but I do expect it will cease to be divided,
>
> It will become all one thing or all the other."

This author believes those words are true today.

CHAPTER 1

Who Are the Two Americas?

In the 2008 presidential primaries, John Edwards, then presidential hopeful, introduced us to the term *Two Americas*. Looking back to the hotly contested 2012 presidential election, the Two Americas were the essential debate. The contention existed in the promises of the various candidates; however, the underlying tension that drove the debates was that the candidates represented two dramatically different pictures of America's past and present. Their suggestions for America's future would be equally dramatically opposed. It is time we discover the roots of the division that Mr. Edwards introduced us to in 2008 and learn how they played a crucial part in directing the outcome of the 2012, 2016, and 2020 elections. This may give us perspective on the explosive 2020 election.

The commentators on the Right speak increasingly of the Progressive movement in America. They hail back to Woodrow Wilson, Teddy Roosevelt, and Lyndon Johnson as leaders of the Progressive movement and suggest that the division in America exists in the political structure. The Right, who oppose Progressive political policies, suggest the alternative to Progressive is Conservative, and that the differences are reflected in both the size and the scope of government. The 2020 presidential candidates highlighted the heart of this division. The 2020 Democratic convention shunned the name of or reference to God. There were repeated deletions of "Under God" when reciting the Pledge of Allegiance, and some would say that the symbolism of the Democratic Convention opposed God.

From John Dewey to Barack Obama—five days till we complete the fundamental tranformation of America

In contrast, nearly every speaker in the Republican Party spoke of God, referred to Him, or thanked Him. I believe most would say that there was a Christian "flavor" to the convention at large. The prayers were all sincerely given by authentic Christians.

The Progressive movement has restructured our political policies far from the roots of the forefathers. The Progressive political policies were enacted by elected leaders who believed they were representing the character and ideals of the modern American citizen. To be clear, it is the citizens of our nation that are divided. All our modern political and social contentions flow from the divide in our worldview as individual citizens. This book is designed to review the blueprint for the dramatic shift in worldview that has been meticulously instituted since the early 1930s. This shift appears to have now reached the tipping point, where the modern citizen group may overthrow the Founders' worldview. This, then, is the great divide, which we will call Two Americas. The new citizen, fully indoctrinated, is emerging as a world citizen. These citizens have distinct morals, principles, and political views. The new citizen takes an entirely different view of the role of government in the life of the citizen and the role of the citizen in the life of the government. The new culture has been established in America by rigorously instituting the blueprint that you now hold in your hand. The blueprint has been institutionalized in education and law since prior to WWII, and as we near the end of 2021, the revolution is nearly complete.

The Blueprint for a New America:
Humanist Manifesto

Mr. Edwards defined the division as one of economics. President Obama enhanced the discrepancy between the Two Americas by projecting an America of rich White people and those of low economic status of any other race. President Obama reinvigorated a racial divide in America because it would serve his worldview. Race and economics have seemingly been the divide that has created the separate Americas.

To these divisions I pose a simple question: Can people of humble financial circumstance, or of any race in America, discover personal happiness, freedom, and success, or does a life of happiness, freedom, and success belong exclusively to White people of means? A second question would be, How many White people would not fit into the "rich" category?

The Founders believed they had instituted a system that would allow any person to pursue happiness. Were they mistaken? Does happiness belong exclusively to the White and the prosperous under our system of government? This great experiment was to allow each individual to carve out and seek their own happiness. No kings were to rule in America; no lords and ladies were to hold a special station above the populace. We were to be a nation ruled by law. The law was to rule equally over rich and poor, wise and fool alike. No one was to be above the law. Each person, regardless of station or wealth, would be held equally accountable to the law. Equality was dear to Americans, and law was instituted because the Founders were so clear about our human nature. James Madison wrote thus:

> If men were angels, no government would be necessary. If angels were to govern men, neither external nor internal controls on government would be necessary. In framing a government which is to be administered by men over men, the great difficulty lies in this: You must first enable the government to control the governed; and in the next place oblige it to control itself. A dependence on the people is, no doubt, the primary control on the government; but experience has taught mankind the necessity of auxiliary precautions.

Our forefathers attempted to form a government that granted opportunity, which *required individual* responsibility but never ensured *outcomes*.

All Citizens Are Equal under the Law

Slavery was the grievous sin of the Founders. For this sin, our nation and its citizens, of all races, have paid a dear price in blood and treasure through the Civil War and the ongoing division and unrest since its abolition. Burke Davis, in *The Civil War: Strange and Fascinating Facts*, claims that the loss of life was a staggering seven hundred thousand people. The evil of racism remained implanted in the hearts and minds of some people long after slavery was made illegal. The philosophy that allowed men to enslave other men must be unveiled here. Slavery was rooted in a perception that some men are naturally of higher quality than others, and as such, they are due the special privilege of a "ruling class." These same individuals who viewed themselves as rulers further believed that there was a need for some to be ruled over. This disposition is crucial to identify as we move forward. The ruling class believed they were above the law and could manipulate the law for their own ends because of their natural privilege. They maintained their privilege through power, wealth, and governmental manipulation. In common practice, some maintained it just through coarse, evil behavior toward others.

The topic of slavery fills volumes, but I recently heard a brilliant interview where Jack Hibbs conversed with Charlie Kirk. Charlie discussed the history of slavery, which I felt was beautifully done. He did not attempt to whitewash the topic or make excuses. He did state facts that I had never heard before and were very enlightening. I recommend you listen to it.

Our nation's story portrays the struggle between the constitutional citizen and the citizen who believes in a ruling class. The constitutional citizen believes that their rights are self-evident since they have been granted to them by their Creator. In turn, they believe it is right to grant some limited power to a small body of people, who then manage limited issues to keep an orderly society and maintain the citizens' rights to pursue happiness, liberty, and life. The constitutional citizens have always been in direct conflict with the elite citizens, who, in their heart, believe that they know what is best for all. Elite citizens consider it their right to rule over others with absolute and unquestioned power and authority in order to form a more perfect world. This struggle between the elitist and the constitutional citizen was at the heart of the slavery issue, and there is little doubt in my mind that today, in this final battle, we are engaged in the same national struggle with a slightly different face.

Hearkening back to James Madison, we see that the struggle existed at the founding of the nation. He noted that not only must the governed be controlled but also that the government must control itself. The checks-and-balances form of government was meant to ensure that government would not get out of control.

Checks and Balances Designed to Thwart a Ruling Class

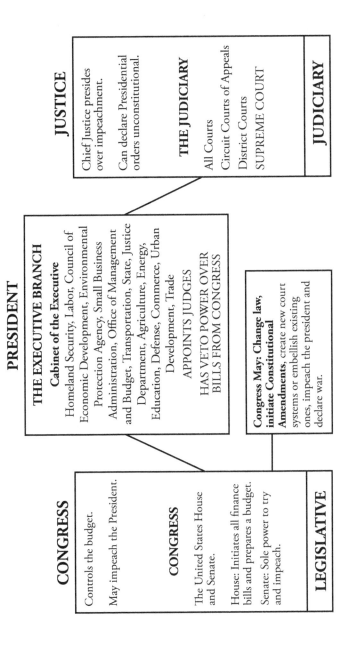

PRESIDENT

JUSTICE

Chief Justice presides over impeachment.

Can declare Presidential orders unconstitutional.

THE JUDICIARY

All Courts
Circuit Courts of Appeals
District Courts
SUPREME COURT

JUDICIARY

THE EXECUTIVE BRANCH

Cabinet of the Executive

Homeland Security, Labor, Council of Economic Development, Environmental Protection Agency, Small Business Administration, Office of Management and Budget, Transportation, State, Justice Department, Agriculture, Energy, Education, Defense, Commerce, Urban Development, Trade

APPOINTS JUDGES

HAS VETO POWER OVER BILLS FROM CONGRESS

Congress May: Change law, initiate Constitutional Amendments, create new court systems or embellish existing ones, impeach the president and declare war.

CONGRESS

Controls the budget.

May impeach the President.

CONGRESS

The United States House and Senate.

House: Initiates all finance bills and prepares a budget.

Senate: Sole power to try and impeach.

LEGISLATIVE

The Three Branches of our Federal Government: The Executive, Legislative, and Judicial have checks and balances over each other. Each have an ability to confirm or deny the acts of the others.

Prejudice has been a tool used to subjugate groups of people in the great struggle for power in America. Our national history is replete with stories of ghettos filled not only with Black and Hispanic people but also with Italians (like my family), Germans, Poles, Jews, and Japanese who have struggled through petty prejudice and injustice from fellow Americans. Many have tough life stories that reveal bullying in schools, misuse by industry, and all manner of hard times. However, many of those who started in ghettos ended up with their own homes, companies, and personal wealth. They finished the race with families whom they love, churches, schools, and communities that they have served and made better. The individual stories have become a part of the American fabric. It is a fabric that is glorious and beautiful, woven out of struggle, in a nation where freedom to succeed and freedom to fail are equally possible.

Each group, having suffered long under some amount of discrimination, has come together in this great melting pot formed from cultures and peoples from around the globe. The individual citizen was forged by trial and time to build the character that would make this nation the greatest in the world, and one that people from around the world would long to call home. There existed a freedom of social, cultural, and economic movement little known in any other society. This attraction propelled millions from around the world to legally immigrate here to America. Immigrants, such as my Italian grandparents, came with dreams. They risked everything, including their lives, to come and seek a better future for themselves and their children. When they arrived, they worked and saved and enjoyed their freedoms.

Many citizens in America feel the "dream" potential has changed or is in the midst of a significant change. We must first know the root of the dream, and then we may be able to grasp the source of this metamorphosis.

I believe there is a rather-simple answer for the loss, yet the answer is absent from public discourse. We are going to embark upon the investigation of two documents that reveal the plan for remaking the American mind, soul, spirit, and lifestyle. These citizens who embody the new "mind and soul" are those who, through their precious right of casting an individual ballot, are completing the metamorphosis.

When a builder undertakes a building, whether it is humble or monumental, there is a set of architectural plans. The architect has a concept of the final project and must then necessarily establish each and every detail. The architect takes into consideration the individual disciplines required to complete the task. This detailed type of review is also used when approaching the undertaking of restructuring an entire society.

In order to apprehend the "new national order," we need to take a first step by remembering from whence we came.

America's Founders gathered in Philadelphia in 1776 to begin this great experiment to institute a government where the citizens had maximum freedom and limited power to a governing body to exercise order for those citizens. They declared our independence from Great Britain and, specifically, from the power of King George's rule over them. Their desire was to bring about a society where a man's strength and his success were earned rather than given as his due because of title or aristocracy. This declaration was a great, wise, and brief document that set the stage for our Constitution and for the nation, which is to follow.

Let us consider its first two paragraphs:

> When in the course of Human Events, it becomes necessary for one people to dissolve the political bands which have connected them with another, and to assume among the powers of the earth, the separate and equal station to which the laws of nature and of nature's God entitle them, a decent respect to the opinions of mankind requires that they should declare the causes which impel them to the separation.

> We hold these truths to be self-evident, that all men are created equal, that they are endowed by their Creator with certain unalienable rights; that among these are life,

liberty, and the pursuit of happiness—That to secure these rights, governments are instituted among men; deriving their just powers from the consent of the governed, that whenever any form of government becomes destructive of these ends, it is the right of the people to alter or to abolish it, and to institute new government, laying its foundation on such principles, and organizing its powers in such form, as to them shall seem most likely to effect their safety and happiness.

It is widely accepted that the men who formulated this government were nearly all professing Christians and that the men who were seemingly the least devout in Christian faith yet were well versed in the Bible as a primary source of wisdom and behavior. (See the *Lives of the Signers of the Declaration* by David Barton, or *Rediscovering God in America* by Newt and Callista Gingrich.) It is indisputable that our memorials and the quotes of the Founding Fathers, as well as the laws that were enacted, sprang from men and women both informed by the Bible and dedicated to God. These men wrote, argued, and drew up the governing documents for the nation with a biblical worldview. They identified these truths:

1. As human events unfold, it may become necessary for people to dissolve political bands, which are the structure that connects them to one another.

2. Once those bands are dissolved, the people, having been separated, may establish a separate station, or form of government, that would be equal to the old.

3. Law flows from nature and nature's God, which entitles men to certain rights that, because of their origin, cannot be taken from them.

4. It is right for a people to declare the cause, which requires them to separate themselves from other men.

These men had a precise life philosophy that informed every thought and every governmental ideal. This does not mean that they would all have been in doctrinal agreement with every spiritual principle, but rather that they shared an overriding life philosophy. There were great debates about the details of government best seen in *The Federalist Papers*. On the whole, these men believed that there was a god who ruled in heaven and that man was not only *not* God but also that man was not good and was fallen in nature.

The Nation the Founders Designed

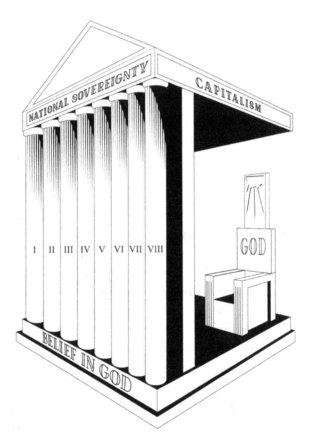

I	Life	V	Liberty and Responsibility
II	Worship of God	VI	Pursuite of Happiness
III	Reliance on God	VII	Limited Government
IV	Rights from God	VIII	Freedom

They would have readily agreed that the Ten Commandments must be part of the framework of the law, because within the Ten Commandments there exists the revelation of man's propensity to do evil and the need to control lawlessness. The Founders designed a government that acknowledged that each citizen, great and small, was equal in the sight of their God and should be treated with equality under the law. The equality, however, did not insinuate equality of personal gifts, ambition, insight, beauty, or talent. The equality was essentially life created by God and given to each individual. A person should be free to live out their gift of life in their own way and to be governed by a system that grants the individual liberty to pursue happiness.

Governments are instituted for the purpose of securing liberty for each citizen; the citizens, in turn, grant the governing authorities limited rule over them in order to retain their freedoms.

Importantly, the next issue the Declaration attends to is the right for citizens, at a time when they believe their government no longer secures these liberties to all, to *abolish* the government, or to alter it, and to institute a new one.

It is apparent that there are now two distinctly different groups of citizens that are growing side by side: *Two Americas* describe us. I would suggest that race and affluence are not dividing lines in our Two Americas. I believe that the Two Americas are made up of citizens who are followers of the Founders' belief and constitutional intent and of the new citizen, who is diametrically opposed to those founding principles. The new citizen desires to abolish the Founders' government, which we have enjoyed, and institute a new one. The difference in the "New American Revolution" is that when our forefathers determined to separate themselves, they followed the Declaration's guidance, which said, "A decent respect to the opinions of mankind requires that they should declare the causes which impel them to separation." Our forefather's Declaration for Independence was literally heard around the world. The declaration for the revolution now in process was begun in a rather quiet fashion but is now roaring like a lion.

The separation we have been undergoing was not declared in a hall in Philadelphia! There were no arms taken up against one another to preserve the old or usher in the new. The two citizens have been living side by side as a slow and quiet revolution has moved forward to replace the Founders' government and our institutions. There was, however, an initial declaration, and then a second declaration. These two documents outlined the specific change that was to be instituted within the population. These documents would give form and direction so that the Progressive political institutions could flow forth as the individual citizen began to shift away from the Founders' worldview and on to the Progressive worldview. Hence progressivism was the expression for the change that was happening on a much more fundamental level.

The questions that must follow are, what are the documents? Where are they? Are they hidden away from view? Why haven't they been declared in the open and thus decided upon with "the respect to the opinions of mankind," as suggested in the Declaration?

The document the Founders wrote secured great freedom; the citizens could have certain expectations while living under that document. The citizens knew that life could bring storms, drought, destruction, enemy attack, famine, disease, death, and uncertainty on any level. They did not look to government to change life circumstances or to solve life's problems. They formed a government that gave the citizen the ability to freely handle what came. There was a foundational principle to this life philosophy, that neighbor would help neighbor, and the government was to allow them the freedom to rally and move forward. Their reliance was placed in themselves and on God. Many citizens were well aware of, and clung to, the promises in the Bible in order to be sustained in a world where there are no guarantees for happiness or health.

These citizens did not wish for the government to define or provide their happiness for themselves, or for their children. They wished the freedom to pursue it *personally* and *financially*, from which sprung forth the free enterprise economic system. They wished to pass on the fruits of their labor to their children and their children's children. Underlying this freedom was the freedom to succeed wildly and the freedom to fail miserably. In both was the tension that those who succeeded could go on to lose everything and those who were failures once could turn their life and fortunes around. The government was to facilitate the individual to explore their own abilities.

The Founders were steeped in the wisdom of the Proverbs. They believed that industry, thrift, charity, humility, and courage were to be the very fiber of their being. The responsibility toward their family was to reflect their fealty to God. Not all the people were serious and industrious, but those who had financial success generally were. The written histories tell of how they handled hardship with patience, and success with humility. They expected little from their government except protection from foreign entities, evil people who would rob and steel from them, and a national mail delivery system.

The Founders' government occasionally meted out certain spectacular opportunities, such as the Homestead Act. This gift of land was not bequeathed out of government largesse but done for the good of the nation, as this governmental decision would ultimately propel the citizens forward to settle the Western territories. Those who received from the government ultimately bore all the risks and would reap any gains. They were free to succeed or fail with no guarantees.

The Founders' government did not behave as a benevolent father gifting a son but as a father who designed opportunities for its citizens. This added strength to the nation as a whole. These citizens hoped for the cavalry to arrive and protect them from vicious, hostile forces. They hoped that the local sheriff could protect them against marauding outlaws who would steal their property or harm their persons. They did not, however, have an expectation of government controlling other circumstances, such as how many ounces of soda they could drink or by what pronoun to address someone or whether they would be forced to wear a mask to buy a gallon of milk even if they were a full six feet from any other shopper the entire time.

This portrayal of government's role in the life of the individual may seem simplistic; however, as the complexity of the society grew, so did the laws and regulations to govern it. Laws grew out of the commonly felt need for order. The citizenry continued to feel that they could control their destiny, knowing some would fail and some would succeed. They knew well that not all who succeeded were good men, and those at the bottom were not, of necessity, bad or shiftless men. Time and chance happen to us all!

The citizen that Woodrow Wilson and Teddy Roosevelt envisioned with their changes in education and law is the humanist citizen of today. The citizen of the 1930s prior to the public indoctrination with humanism is substantially different from the one transformed by secular humanism. Their relationship to the government, and their expectations of government, consists of a list of rights. This new citizen happily turns over his destiny and much of his freedom in exchange for hope in the power of government to fulfill his basic needs. The new citizens believe that they have the right to receive food, clothing, education, shelter, a minimum income, medical care, transportation, and retirement care out of the supposed endless common government largesse. The theist citizen of the 1930s would never have embraced this view of his liberty.

The new humanist citizen expects government to provide many personal comforts; the constitutional citizen wants freedom from government interference.

Humanists expect government to provide the following:

- Food
- Shelter
- Insurance for health, work, catastrophe
- Education
- Basic income

Framework for the Humanist Citizen's Government

I	State Free of Religion	V	Will of Elite Collective
II	Trust in Government	VI	Abortion & Euthanasia
III	Situational Ethics	VII	Value Based Education
IV	Limited Rights	VIII	Sexual License

An accurate picture of this new citizen can be seen in the movie *The Truman Show*. This movie, starring Jim Carrey, depicts the first person who was purchased in utero by a corporation. The corporate head becomes the complete unquestioned director and final authority of the "true man's" life. To this true man, the director is God. Carrey plays Truman, and the cameras never leave him. While the entire world watches his life on TV, every need is met, including a wife, friends, job, car, house, food, and leisure. Every aspect of his life is completely controlled by his owner. He is kept safe, is fed, and his time is fully directed. He never meets conflict, pain, suffering, disappointment, a bully, or a hypocrite. He does not know war, famine, heartache, or religion. He believes that he is a free man to do as he wants, until the time that he begins to exercise his freedoms. He then quickly discovers that he has *never* been free! Slowly the truth dawns that he is being held captive in his life's role. He continues to question his existence and suspects that there is more. As Truman searches for his freedom, his captor-owner and director of the film is frustrated by Truman's rebellion against the omnipotent wisdom and power he wields over Truman's life. He is like God for Truman, but completely unlike the God revealed in the Bible and believed in by millions. The God of the Bible allows bad things to happen because, first and foremost, He has granted mankind free will. Certainly, we see His intervention in our lives, and many can see how He has saved them from peril, but He does not take our free will. This human filmmaker and controller is the opposite of the biblical God, because he demands complete, unquestioned control and only gives the *illusion* of free will. Truman is actually given a limited free will, which is subordinated to the exclusive will of the elite man who owns him.

The dramatic climax takes place in the man-made ocean where Carry fights in a man-made storm for his life. His owner toys with the idea of drowning him rather than allowing him to be free. The citizen's battle for their personal liberty is no less dramatic and no less serious. It appears that those who now hold power would consent to destroy the country rather than allow the citizens to take back their rightful position under God's control, rather than man's.

Free will is a living principle in the Founders' documents and reflects their faith in the God of the Bible. This aspect of freedom is one of the essential differences between the Founders' government and the humanist doctrines, as we will see as we study the documents line upon line.

In the humanist government model, the governing agencies take on the role of benevolent dictators, and while the citizenry sees themselves as expectant children, the ruling class sees them as slaves. It is a precise picture of the slavery model discussed earlier. The elite regard themselves to be a superior class of humans who deeply believe it is best for them to control and allot the world's goods to its people. In the event that there are natural disasters, such as storms, famine, or disease, they will provide and protect. In the event of death, accident, sickness, an unfair employer, or a nasty neighbor, the government will step in and determine fealty. The citizens under this form of government see the government as an omniscient God with unlimited wisdom and resources to meet any need. Considering government as omniscient, it follows that government should control all natural resources and all wealth in order to distribute as it sees fit.

The goal of this book is to fully explore the *Humanist Manifesto I* and the *Humanist Manifesto II*, with the idea of observing how they have been instituted in our nation and how they have changed the individual citizen's worldview as well as the social structure. We will look at each specific affirmation, in both documents, and explore briefly the authors of the documents. These two documents make up the architectural plan for the citizen of 2021 and beyond.

If you sense that there is a growing tension between the two groups, you are not wrong! These philosophies are diametrically opposed to each other. The time has come to identify the clashing principles each holds so that we can either embrace one and shun the other or openly recognize the battle that is being waged so it can be brought to the public forum for discussion.

The first tenet of *Humanist Manifesto I*, written in 1933, is, **"Religious humanists regard the universe as self-existing and not created."**

We will explore more fully the effects of instituting atheism in exchange for a Judeo-Christian worldview at a later time, but first, let us look at the sixth tenet of the first manifesto, which reads, "We are convinced that the time has passed for theism, deism, modernism and the several varieties of 'new thought.'"

The second manifesto reiterates that there is no God but affirms a "new" spiritual nature, encouraging spiritual experiences and aspirations apart from God.

Humanism not only disagrees with the existence of God but also steps into an adversarial role with theists. This is seen in the second tenet of the second manifesto, which reads, *"Promises of immortal salvation or fear of eternal damnation are both illusory and harmful. They distract humans from present concerns, from self actualization and from rectifying social injustices."*

The humanist does not just envision their philosophy as different and alternative to the Founding Fathers'; he believes that a government based on belief in God is harmful. He addresses our free enterprise economy when we read thus in the fourteenth affirmation of *Humanist Manifesto I*:

> The humanists are firmly convinced that existing acquisitive and profit-motivated society has shown itself to be inadequate, and that a radical change in methods, controls, and motives, must be instituted. A socialized and cooperative economic order must be established to the end that the equitable distribution of the means of life is possible. The goal of humanism is a free and universal society in which people *voluntarily* [italics mine] and intelligently cooperate for the common good. Humanists *demand a shared life in a shared world* [italics mine].

With just this taste of the blueprint for change, let me stop for a moment and broadly describe the world from the humanist perspective as we see in just these three tenets.

1. The society would be purely secular; no vestiges of belief in a salvation-providing God who hears prayer would be present. All sects of Christianity and Judaism must be silenced or eliminated. The humanist does not just disagree with the belief in a god who saves from the possibility of damnation; they state that these beliefs are harmful!

2. Capitalism is replaced with Socialism.

3. The necessity of redistribution requires the development of two groups: the elites, who exist outside and above the law and above the general population, and the masses. In our early days as a nation, these were called slaves and slave owners.

4. All resources of the world are shared (one-world government). Nations must relinquish their sovereignty, and the United States, as the most powerful nation in the world, must be first to do so.

5. There must be a need that is felt by the people and which government may use to control them. Environmentalism and global warming act as the vehicle to bring about increased government control.

6. An illusion of freedom exists (think Truman), but it does not extend to traditional spiritual beliefs, which would include marriage, legal promise of life, or gender differentiation.

7. The children must be controlled in order to raise a generation fully indoctrinated to be the citizen of the future. The public education system will be used to indoctrinate, not instruct!

8. The one-world secular (atheist) state is ushered in.

The specifics of how to achieve this brave new world are found in the documents that we will study. The Founders, while unquestionably Christian, gave us a government in which the citizens had freedom of religion, not freedom *from* religion. Secular humanism seeks to install one national religion, thereby removing freedom of religion from us; however, they utilize the argument of "separation of church and state" in the courts to remove all vestiges of Christianity, creating a nation *free* of theistic religion. Each individual was granted the freedom to shape their own doctrinal beliefs, but they would have expected the society to work within the wisdom expressed in the Bible. The humanists are putting into place laws and social practices that are entirely intolerant of our Founders' faith and in striking opposition to biblical admonitions.

This, then, outlines the Two Americas as I define them. I believe that each of the Americas is made up of rich and poor, of Black, White, Brown, Yellow, and Red. I further believe that race and economic status have little to do with the division, which has created an ongoing environment of animosity between these Two Americas.

There are Americans who may have no church affiliation yet retain a core belief that there is a God in the universe and that they are not this god! Some believe He walks beside them and speaks to them from the pages of the Bible. Some believe that He is impersonal and has set the world spinning and stood back to watch what will happen. At their core, these citizens concur that the rights as citizens in the United States of America have emanated forth from God and that, as such, their rights should not be taken from them.

Other citizens, rich and poor, Black, White, Brown, Yellow, and Red, also believe deeply that there is *no* God, and they look to government to provide, protect, and manage all resources so that each will have an equal share. They believe that government should be the managing force that controls and redistributes wealth, chooses the businesses that will succeed and those that will fail, decides what job they and their children will best fit within, and provides the education that will prepare the citizen for his work in the overall "hive." They see themselves not as individuals responsible to God but as part of a collective to be directed. They believe that home, food, medical care, and clothing should be provided by the government. These citizens believe that the government should be responsible for the raising of children and provision of childcare. This is the new citizen of 2021 and beyond. I would hope that this little book could help citizens identify which side of this divide they occupy.

The Two Americas, I posit, are much more radically different from the divisions others have suggested. I invite you to step into these pages and see if you agree with me.

CHAPTER 2

The Big Changes

The flood of social change comes at an overwhelming pace today. I have suggested to my husband that I feel like I am being waterboarded. *Waterboarding* is a method of torture where one feels like they are drowning at the hands of an unmerciful adversary. One evidently gasps occasionally for air, and the captor allows enough air to sustain life, but never so much as to suggest that the torture will subside.

The constant flow of radical change is an everyday occurrence. I could detail each day for a month here below and the book would be much larger but would not accomplish my purpose. If you are a citizen who agrees with the Founders, you will notice the day-to-day flow of radical change that you feel drowned in. You will perceive how people in high places of authority fail to obey the basic laws of the land with no consequences. You will notice the apparent double standard that exists for anyone in government that is perpetuating the new world order, as opposed to the Founders' principles. You will have to agree that the ruling class lives above the law while the slave class is subject to increasingly severe law, regulation, and restriction.

Consider General Michael Flynn, who suffered through three years of the harassment of the FBI over charges that documents have disclosed they never felt he was guilty of. Following the document drop that proved his innocence, the attorney general of the United

States, Bill Barr, told the justice department to drop all charges because they were bogus. While Flynn was proclaimed innocent by the justice department, still the judge who tried his case has decided to also become the prosecutor and is demanding a new trial. This level of new "elite class" who controls every breath a citizen takes and can ruin lives on trumped-up, false charges is breathtaking, but it will be commonplace in the new humanist world. General Michael Flynn's torture was only brought to a halt because of a presidential pardon.

The foundational changes are vast, yet only a few elites could have envisioned them seventy years ago. As I write this small book, I remember back to the Democratic convention of 2012, where amazingly the party platform came out without a single reference to God, nor did it acknowledge the existence of Israel. This, even for the Democratic Party, represents a change of immense proportions. Their platform focused heavily upon the social transformation that they hope to accomplish. At a time when our nation's economy is failing, debt is skyrocketing, the education system is falling far behind those of other nations of the world, unrest is exploding in America, and a threat with North Korea and China is growing, the Democratic Party is almost entirely focused on support for gay, lesbian, transvestite, and bisexual marriage, women in combat, the Black Lives Matter movement, removing police departments, and global warming! Why, you may ask, is this the focus? The answer is clear—because the social structure is where the final work must be done to complete the transition away from the theist citizens' worldview.

The national party who wins the 2020 election will be the party who will be able to address this great divide. Should the theists be able to sit in the seats of power, they may be able to reclaim some ground that has been lost. They will only gain ground if the battle is *defined*, which is the sole purpose of this book.

We will not explore the elimination of God in our nation. There is no longer a debate about the aggressive movement to eliminate God from our public and, to whatever extent possible, from our private lives. It is no longer a debate that the war on God in America is a war directed at Christians primarily (of all sects) and secondarily at Jews. We might broadly term both groups as "people of *the* book." The overall war on God in America is currently part of our national discourse, and the facts surrounding the litigation are being detailed by many current authors and are indisputable. I would suggest Phyllis Schlafly's latest book *No Higher Power* as a beginning, and then Ann Coulter's *Godless*. Our goal here is to read and understand the written plan that is being followed to institute the secular state in our nation and to ascertain how effective the implementation has been.

As we examine the *Humanist Manifesto*, we challenge individual readers to thoughtfully examine their own worldview. We must soon affirm our allegiance to one direction or another for America. *No individual legislator can alter our course now.* The course we take for the future will be directed by individual citizens. The way the individual citizen thinks, lives their lives, instructs their children, and finally, vote for their representatives will guide and direct us. Make no mistake: we, individual citizens, must take a look at where the master plan is leading us. We are on our way to a new world, and we must wake up. Choose the new world with eyes open by selecting the current direction, or with eyes open, help restore the foundations of America. In either case, once you travel these pages, you will indeed know how we got on this train and where it is taking us.

The Two Americas are being ripped to shreds. We have become so deeply weak that we are becoming ripe for a takeover. The humanist will welcome it, for as long as the US stands strong, they will not be able to fulfill their worldwide plans. Contrarily, the moment the US falls, it will be a short time until the world is in their hands.

The Individual Citizen Will
Determine If We Remain Free

The Third Reich in Power by Richard J. Evans is a most instructive book about the means and methods used in transforming the German culture. He quotes Joseph Goebbels speaking on November 15, 1933 (p. 120). Goebbels was speaking of art but addressed the revolution:

> "The revolution we have made is a total one. It has encompassed every area of public life and fundamentally restructured them all. It has completely changed and reshaped people's relationships to each other, to the state

and questions of existence." This was, he went on, a "revolution from below," driven on by the people, because, he said, it had brought about the transformation of the German nation into one people. Becoming one people meant establishing a unity of spirit across the nation, for as Goebbels had already announced in March: "On 30 January the era of individualism finally died… The individual will be replaced by the community of the people." "Revolutions," he added, "never confine themselves to the purely political sphere. From there they reach out to cover all other areas of human social existence. The economy and the culture, science and scholarship, and art are not protected from their impact." There could be no neutrals in this process: no one could stand aside under false claims of objectivity, or art for art's sake. For, he declared: "Art is no absolute concept; it only gains life from the life of the people." Thus: There is no art without political bias.

The German people, mesmerized by a new idea and controlled by a media who fed them state-determined propaganda, fell into lockstep for a time.

America read of the curse that had come on Europe and, for many reasons, entered into the fray, giving life and treasure to save these faraway lands from whence many American families were rooted.

The history of that horrific time is still available, but the people who lived it are quickly fading, and now the memory of the system that spawned unthinkable atrocities is being forgotten or even misremembered by this generation. WWII, with its destruction, devastation, and death, would not be so real and so terrifying for me had my father, who risked his life to help stop the monster and preserve America's freedom, not reminded our family of the threat. Dad kept us aware that our freedoms were bought with a price. He reminded us that the abundant opportunities of America are not available everywhere.

We thought America would remain free, prosperous, and full of opportunity forever, but for the last thirty years, we have seen the stranglehold of intolerance cripple our nation. We have seen freedom disintegrate and a national/state religion put into place which undermines our institutions, laws, and personal lives. The nation has changed before our eyes to an intolerance we would never have thought possible. We can nearly say, like Joseph Goebbels, that the revolution is total and has encompassed every area of life and culture.

In 2012, President Obama made a promise to his constituents that he, with their support, would fundamentally transform America. The transformation was already in progress. He was actually hoping to preside over the final movement of the citizenry, away from our foundational belief in limited government with God-secured freedoms. The exchange away from the Founders' government to the new humanist one-world government was to be completed in our current president's term. This new citizen will have a completely new relation to the government. A humanist system will grant unlimited power over the citizen, and government will act as final arbiter of all life achievements. The power of this form of government will be undefined in scope and grant unlimited powers to government officials, which are chosen, not elected. It will usher the full elite caste to rule over the slave caste. No longer will there be inalienable rights that we derive from God.

As we look back over the past fifty years, we can agree that the day-to-day changes that technology has made are vast and could not have been foreseen. While these changes affect our day-to-day lives, it is unquestionable that the changes in the fabric of the American people have been even more dramatic than the technology and were equally unforeseen. American life, its families, and its philosophies are drastically different from what they were in 1960. We have progressively redefined *family* and have now redefined *marriage*. Marriage, for thousands of years, has been considered the foundation of the family. In forty years, the family has undergone a metamorphosis. The roles of men and women have changed, the biblical family format having been overturned. The role of children has been greatly altered, and their relationship to the adult population around them has changed. The faith, character, moral limits, and personal aspirations of parents for their children have been completely altered. Social change, then, has a greater consequence than the technology that blossomed forth and secured the change in our generation. The body of law surrounding the environment has burgeoned. Public servants take a great deal of time and national treasure devoted to setting increasing standards that promise safety and security. The outcome of the new citizenry has been to elect elites to public office who promise the safety and security that could, heretofore, only be obtained through diligence and thrift on an individual basis, and also trust in God.

The first *Humanist Manifesto* was written and instituted in 1933. The same year that Joseph Goebbels proclaimed the revolution in Germany was "complete." Through this manifesto, the transformation of our social structure was well orchestrated and fervently executed. Most of our citizens today have no idea where the ideas and philosophies came from that rule the political and social landscape. They have no idea where an entirely new worldview, which diametrically opposes our basic moral constructs, has come from and how it has taken over the public school system.

Those of us who feel the tension building sense that every day more of the structure for the new world order is in place, and less remains of the original intent of our republic. The practical aspects of our lives are literally demolished, while the citizens stand by with helpless resignation. There is an underlying hope that those who are so faithfully dismantling the nation and building the new structure are doing it by accident and don't mean to take our *freedoms*. The great mystery is that freedom is being stripped away by people who say they want *freedom*, and we are increasingly being suffocated by the intolerance of those who proclaim themselves tolerant!

The framework of this intolerance has been placed into law and adopted by custom. But have you wondered "how" the change took place? Have you stopped to ask yourself thus:

1. How did a nation where the people openly and comfortably expressed faith in God become a people where the mention of

God in any public format precipitates a legal action? (Appendix article, 1 by Allen Sears.)

2. How did we exchange Christmas and Easter in the public school for winter and spring Break or even Kwanzas celebrations? (Appendix article 2, by Paul Wilson.)

3. How has the singing of "Silent Night" become banned by the same schools that instruct young children in stretching condoms on zucchini to practice for premarital sex? (See appendix article 3, by Mary Fuchs.)

4. How have a people whose Constitution was formed on rights given by God been bullied into closing the doors of schools, county buildings, and public property to any acknowledgment of the Ten Commandments and of our Judeo-Christian roots? (See appendix article 4, by Callie Woodlief.)

5. How have the public school systems taught as scientific fact the theory of evolution and disallowed any other thoughtful exploration into our beginnings? (See appendix article 5, by Anti-Defamation League.)

6. How could it be that while science continues to reveal the complexity and miraculous nature of all living things, and at a time when increasing numbers of scientists at the highest levels of research begin to postulate Intelligent Design while the public school system disallows any science instruction that would question evolution, to further the prejudice against Intelligent Design, universities have blocked students with a decidedly "design" belief system to advance in degrees in the sciences? (See *Expelled* by Ben Stein.)

7. How has the public's greatest treasure, their children, become increasingly less educated at a continually higher cost to the taxpayer? (See appendix article "The Education Notebook: The

Cost of American Education," by the Heritage Foundation.)

8. Why do our public school graduates know so much less about the history of Western civilization, geography, math, science, art, and music than in times past? (See appendix article by Diane Ravitch.)

9. How can reporters terrorize the public, and teachers terrorize schoolchildren, with the fear of environmental catastrophe, when even the most casual research reveals natural disaster has been a common thread throughout all of recorded history. (See *Climategate* by Brian Sussman, and *The Mad, Mad, Mad World of Climatism: Mankind and Climate Change Mania* by Steve Goreham.)

10. How is it that politicians say they speak for you, The American people, in generalities that do not fit any people you know?

11. Do you wonder what educational purpose the state of California has for teaching homosexual heroes for kindergarteners and bringing transgender information to the same age group?

12. Do you question the wisdom and purpose of a California law which prohibits parents from obtaining counseling for their minor children that would include a biblical and health perspective regarding their feelings toward members of the same sex? (See appendix article "California's Gay Reparative Therapy Ban Faces Legal Test.")

If you have asked yourself these questions, you must know, there is a plan. What was once a slow-moving giant has become a daily barrage of change that is truly breathtaking. One scarcely knows what to try to save. Many citizens just shake their heads in unbelief and quietly sit down as it overtakes them. Each of the above situations makes perfectly good sense if you are a citizen locked into the revolution. They are heartbreaking for the citizen who mirrors the Founders' thoughts. We may now feel we reside in an upside-down world. My one sanity is to understand how this has come about, and to anticipate what the new world order's main priorities are. This gives some small amount of order to the demolition around me. We are about to engage in the rules for the new world order right out of the rule book; it is my hope you will have your eyes forever opened to the atheist plan for the world. Soon we will all know what we must do and become and affirm in order to stop this process in its path and begin to turn the ship back. If we choose to do nothing, we will learn to live quietly without frustration in the new, fundamentally restructured America.

Many have scoffed when the term war on values was introduced some thirty years ago. There was an outcry that it was the prudish outlook of born-again Christians that was at fault. We heard about the "war on families" and, most recently, the "war on marriage." This revolution is being fought in the emotional spotlight of the media and behind the closed doors of courtrooms. The strategy has been to rely on name-calling. *Bigot, intolerant, homophobe* are just three that are well used. Traditional values are continually brought before the court system to be defeated. Those things that the general public would never allow to travel through the House and Senate will find themselves in the courts system and where the precedent of judicial proceedings "create the law." The use of the courts has been the primary method of establishing secular humanism. It was the courts that banned prayer in schools; it was not an act of the legislature. It is the courts that have eliminated Christmas, allowed statues to be torn down, given "special privilege" status to people who are gay or lesbian or transgender. This is all new law formed in the court.

It is crucial that theists understand the new state religion and the power it wields in order to evaluate their place within the social structure.

CHAPTER 3

Wilder than Fiction

California University (1970–1975)

Please be patient while I take you on a little side trip. It is a very personal rabbit trail about my own university days, and it is very important to visit the halls of the university during this period before we hit the "meat" of our discussion. This information is completely germane, and yet very personal. It adds perspective to recognize that you and I have been part of this very dramatic historic movement. I am about to take you inside of a university campus of the 1970s where the citizens for this revolutionary army were being prepared.

The experience that I will describe belonged to me but was not uncommon. My university experience was likely similar for the West Coast university system and explains the voting records and the wide acceptance of humanism expressed by college graduates from 1960 on. The 1975 graduating class from a Northern California university turned out students thoroughly indoctrinated in the new social order. I was one of them. Some specifics of the educational experience are well worth examining, not because of the wonderful quality education provided, but for the systematic coordination of indoctrination across most of the disciplines.

The beautiful, stately campus was, like most institutions of higher learning, filled with lofty, lovely buildings, manicured grounds, a huge library, and most of all, young people who were convinced their parents knew nearly nothing about what was taking place in the classrooms or on the campus. The students were quite accurate in this one area.

In every direction and in every department, there was a professor that I set myself to impress. We wanted to succeed and to make a difference in the world. This was a time of demonstrations, protests, long Rastafarian hair, tie-dyed T-shirts, braless women, and shirtless men.

The students were offspring of the generation who fought a war and returned home to use their GI Bill, go to college, and then enter a vibrant workforce. The WWII generation were of the parents of the students at my university. Many of those parents were the first from their families to graduate from college. Their country and families were very proud of them. This World War II generation wanted the same and more for their children. They wanted the prestige of college educations and the preparation for their children to do well in the workforce. The WWII generation had worked hard and began to amass the good life provided by our industrial revolution. In the acquisition of wealth came the plan for university education for their children. Not many of my peers used loans to get through college; most were either self-supporting or supported by their parents' efforts. My dad happened to have remained in the Air Force as a "lifer," so we had a unique experience of traveling back and forth across the country, changing schools, homes, communities, and friends fairly regularly. Our parents did not believe university was essential, but they did not discourage it.

We must take a sideward move to Arizona, where I spent my freshman year, and then we will return to the details of California. My freshman year was spent at a very conservative university in northern Arizona. I was a declared English major but was fascinated with philosophy. My Catholic upbringing had instilled a set of values that I had begun to question late in high school. Those values would not come under serious question, however, until my introduction to the freshman course of ethics. It was shortly after my first semester of ethics that my Catholic training began to topple. I can't say that I remember all the people we studied, but I can say that by the end of my first semester, one thing was certain: I had been taught that each individual was responsible for establishing their own set of ethical values and principles which would guide their life. There were no longer absolutes. Not so subtle in the classroom was the inference that our parents' generation did not know much and that it was our responsibility for the *future* of mankind. We were the great ones; we were the hope to *change* the world (the hope and change of 2008 was really nothing new). We were taught the only "truth" in the universe is that there is no truth and that there is *no* God. We were instructed that we were our only authority. It should not come as a surprise that many students experimented with drugs—they did not consider this experimentation to be wrong. They knew their parents disagreed, but considered their parents' values old-fashioned.

In my spare time, and for fun, I tried out for a play, got a part, and was recruited onto the costume crew because of my sewing skills. The commitment to the performance meant that free time and friends were mostly theater arts majors, radio and communications students, as well as English majors. They were a colorful and fun bunch; many came from wealthy homes. Their wealth and disrespect of their parents' hard work was new to me. I was from a by-the-blue-book military family with little extra money and no room for disrespect. This was my first step into 1970s college education.

I should note here, just for clarity and to shed light on the historic timeline, that boys lived in male dorms, girls in female dorms. The boys had to check in at the front desk for a date and wait in the lobby till we came down to meet them. A dorm mother checked our rooms on Friday late afternoon, and if the room was not spotless, and the floor clean and shining, you did not have the privilege of going out that weekend. No social life without domestic order! There were hard-and-fast rules, and this was a state institution.

While the dorm rooms had order, the rest of the campus was a laboratory of completely new ideas and behaviors. The heroes and role models were all new and at odds with my upbringing. It was in my freshman year when I was introduced to the homosexual culture. Many of the boys in the theater group were homosexuals, and I was to discover that one of the primary professors in the Theater Arts Department was also gay and threw wild parties with the boys at his house. It was presumed that everyone thought it was just fine. There was a prejudice, if you will, against anyone who did not conform to thinking homosexuality was cool.

I clearly remember a day when a friend in a play came to me and told me that his sister was going to commit suicide because the girl whom she was "in love with" had rejected her and would not accommodate her lesbian advances. Up until this time in my life, I had been completely unaware of this lifestyle. I am not certain I even knew what homosexuality was until being faced with it in college. My experience was not unique. While students who were in science and math majors might have experienced far less indoctrination than I did, in the humanities, everyone was being manipulated and everyone was put on the same "train track" heading for a humanist utopia. Rebellion from the parental morals and religious training was common, as were drugs. One of my roommates had to leave school because her main course every day was marijuana. She had come from a very privileged New York family. She listened to very dark music, was unhappy all the time, and spent remarkable sums of her parents' money on horrendous clothes that made her look like a dark waif. I suspect that her story is repeated day in and day out in colleges all over the country even today. Psychology books were everywhere, and college students held their parents accountable for their horrible problems, for the problems of pollution, for the problems of war and famine. It was not a very uplifting place to be. The division between the learned college student and his unsophisticated parents was stark. The concepts of fallen man and sin nature were completely removed. In whatsoever way a student was ill equipped or unhappy, the root of the problem was inevitably the repressed or evil childhood experiences.

My sophomore year built upon the foundation that was established in Arizona. I moved to Northern California to finish my degree at the university there.

Traveling north along the California coast, one eventually leaves all the big cities and sprawling freeways behind and enters into the dark narrow patch of highway that winds its way through the Avenue of the Giants. Once there, one realizes they have entered a place on earth that is otherworldly. The latent power of these enormous redwood trees standing in the primeval forest literally stuns the imagination. The canopy of branches completely darkens the ground below. It is covered in cool shade, with occasional delicate streams of sunlight that make their way to earth and speak volumes to the beholder. The delicate floras that thrive in the shade of these beautiful trees are rich, lacy ferns, huge skunk cabbages with sprawling lily-like white flowers, and a carpet of other lovely, delicate flowers in yellow and violet. The sound in this ancient forest is like nowhere I had ever been before—it is utterly still. The thick forest debris, along with the bushy bark, completely absorbs any wayward sound. You can hear the stillness of your own breathing, your own thoughts. I sat on a piece of an ancient downed log at nineteen and considered that I was forever changed. The fragrance of the forest, the power and imagination in the detail of the creation, and the power of complete silence wrote upon my soul a message that would help me overcome the indoctrination of the university to which I was heading. The truth in the power and majesty of creation, which far surpassed the accident of evolution, was indelibly impressed upon my soul. Should one ever need to bring their soul to a place that is utterly still, they need only travel to this redwood forest, where all worldly sound is absorbed by the forest and a new "sound" emerges. It is the sound of pure silence, a peace beyond description, and as I mentioned before, it is otherworldly.

As a college student passing through these rich forests, I was mesmerized. The stark desert with stunning mountains, saguaro, and cholla cacti had been my home. Before making the trip out to California, I had researched the North Coast, its history, flora, fauna, and industry, but nothing in a book could have prepared me for the sights and sounds of the forest that day. As I drove into Eureka on my way to my destination, I passed a huge logging truck that had a full load with one part of one tree. The awe of the living forest was fresh in my mind, so watching this downed tree on its way to market was a sight that primed me for the environmental bandwagon I was about to jump onto once I reached the university.

The campus was built at the foot of a similarly large and awe-inspiring redwood forest. Since we have such a young country, we do not have buildings that mark the passing of generations as they do in Europe, but here in these forests, for the first time, for many students and for me, the certainty of the passing of time, the disappearance of generations of people, and the civilizations passing became evident. It was akin to traveling into prehistoric times, where civilization stood still and the forests grew around them.

The campus was located in a small quaint university town. In its earlier days, it was likely that this campus prepared teachers and forest rangers. Now it was a gathering place for hippies from all over the United States. The coast was almost always a cold, steel gray. The sky often matched the gray of the ocean, but when the sun was out and the sky was blue, it was probably one of the most beautiful places on earth.

It was 1972, and I was excited to get into college and explore life. The college was buzzing with political activism. The students wanted to save the redwood forests, get out of Vietnam, and change the political structure and liberate women. Richard Nixon was president and wildly unpopular on the campus. He was known for his anti-Communist position and, as a politician, was transferring power away from the federal government in Washington and back to the states. These were unpopular opinions at that time. I was entirely unschooled in anything political but passionate to have the world be a better place! We were "flower children." We listened to Simon and Garfunkel and had huge Renaissance festivals filled with booth after booth of homemade candles, leatherwork, jewelry, pottery, and the like. There was a desire to turn from the industrial revolution and get back to a simpler life with the earth. We knew that political action was necessary, but in our ignorance of the Founding Fathers, and of the consequence of destroying or replacing their ideas, we became useful idiots for the revolutionaries that knew exactly where they wanted to take our nation.

Sometime early in the first semester, an English professor (during class time) introduced the class to transcendental meditation. He was probably in his late forties and was the very sage of all wisdom—we all thought he was cool. He posited that anyone who regularly meditated would be more peaceful and that the answer to obtain world peace was in our hands, by becoming part of the transcendental meditation movement. He suggested that those who meditated had better mental acuity and would get better grades. He invited all students to a lecture at the university that evening. After the evening session, further describing the benefits in meditation, and being a student who sought peace, joy, and good grades, I decided to go through the induction process.

Those students who wanted to begin their life of meditation were to go to his home on the weekend. The instruction for the induction was to bring a fruit offering to the gods, and I was set for a time to go to his home along with many other students.

I have no idea what college students of 2021 are like, but the college students of 1971 were at once incredibly arrogant and abominably ignorant. We had a certainty that we knew more than our parents, but were not only ignorant but also foolish on almost every level. Unfortunately, our attitude assumed that we had a self-appointed right to rule the world. We were pampered, self-indulgent children in adult bodies. We were called "hippies," and many of us were truly searching for something more in life than we saw in our parents, who were devoted to Capitalism and the American way. We were looking for something to fill a spiritual void, and since many of us had rejected the spiritual roots of our childhood, transcendental meditation seemed as though it might be a fit. The proselytizing of the university professors was open and aggressive.

In case you are unaware of the ceremony that surrounds transcendental meditation induction, I want to give you a small peek. There is a brief ceremony where the inductee brings their fruit offering before a statue (which, sometime later, I realized was a pagan god), and candles. A commitment is spoken, and then you are given a mantra, which you are obligated to keep secret. Once you have a mantra, you are taught to use it to take you to a deeper state of meditation. For success, you are instructed to mediate for twenty to thirty minutes morning and evening. It was many years after this little dedication on that Saturday morning when I comprehended that what I had done was a serious religious act with many implications. We were like sheep being lead to slaughter!

Before my sophomore year had passed, I had been in a communication class that endorsed and supported open marriage (using the book *Open Marriage* as a textbook). This was designed to redefine the basic building block of society (marriage) and move this institution away from the biblical roots of fidelity in marriage and to endorse marriage that included each partner having physical relations with other people at will.

We had many communication exercises designed by the teacher to break down any moral values that were outdated and wrongly instilled by old-fashioned parents. Women's studies mocked the Bible as being filled with evil patriarchs. I had no affiliation to the Bible, so it did not bother me, but it bothered a fellow student whom everyone thought was crazy.

It appeared that *everyone*—including instructors—openly approved of and/or used drugs. Timothy Leary's LSD experimentation was lauded as exploring the unknown. The classroom and personal discussions included readings of Carlos Castaneda and many others like him. It was clear that becoming educated was to discover beyond our current parochial life; the use of drugs was to be part of the discovery process.

I, thankfully, was terrified of drugs, which kept me from joining the experimentation. Unthankfully, I was confused about my moral direction, which caused a couple of years that I consider as lost. After becoming inducted in TM, I began exploring other religions and clearly remember saying out loud to God, "If You are real, I will follow You and obey as I am able, but You must make Yourself known. Otherwise, I will go my own way." Thankfully, God answered that prayer and made Himself known to me.

I never heard an audible voice, but His still small voice began to direct me back to what I now consider rational thought. I questioned evolution, I questioned abortion, and I questioned why in a world of wonderful literature we were assigned such dark and shocking reading in literature classes. It seems a little odd now that I think back, but the transformational grammar class was one of my favorite English classes. I think it was because it was all exacting order in the midst of the moral and intellectual chaos around me.

Included in the required reading for biology class were *The Population Bomb* by Paul Ehrlich and *Silent Spring* by Rachel Carson. These two books established the social setting in which all other biological information would be digested. The Zero Population Club, or ZPG, was headed by an influential, and somewhat charismatic, older Dutch professor. His wife was actively involved in getting Planned Parenthood into the public schools and waging open war with the "untaught masses" who still went to outmoded churches and opposed Planned Parenthood's teaching of sex education to their children. These books and the biology curriculum had the twofold design of making the student feel responsible for the planet, and, secondly, lending a sense of urgency to their activism. We were convinced the planet had a very short time to exist if we did not change things—sound familiar? The visual loss of the mighty redwoods provided an additional impetus to the students at this California university. We actively protested Capitalism (which included agriculture, the lumber industry, the pharmaceutical industry, and big-box stores), marriage, fidelity, and war. This essentially hooked our generation into the "environmental movement." We became the experts, and our parents the dunces who just raped the planet.

As students, we did not question either the wise Dutch professor or his wife's leadership, and so we were drawn into the community battle regarding sex education. Looking back, it is apparent that none of us were taxpayers, most were not parents, and most had no ties to the community; but we were used as pawns to speak against the community members who *were* parents and were attempting to protect their children from the molestation that they saw in Planned Parenthood's view of sex. We adopted the professor and his wife's point of view and reasoned that children were going to have sex so they needed birth control or the world was going to end because of the population explosion.

Much of the community organizing took place in the home of the Dutch biology professor and his wife. Their home was gladly opened to their students and became a hub of activity where likeminded students gathered to insert themselves into causes. This same professor was elected to the city council with the help of the students, and we were able to place a young fellow student into the state legislature, who still serves as a Progressive Democrat today. The "causes" were to bring about the new and better world order. The students were instructed and believed that the planet was going to die because of evil people having babies, killing trees, using paper products, and making profits. People were destroying the environment, and our evil chemicals were destroying all the birds, fish, wildlife, and insects. We were indoctrinated to believe that it was crucial to stop populating in our generation. Pregnancy was considered a disease, not a blessing. We were instilled with the belief that if we did have children, we must be conscientious and have no more than two—zero population growth! We joined the Sierra Club, Zero Population Growth, and supported the ACLU, all with absolutely no comprehension of what the political power in the hands of these organizations would look like thirty years hence. We were taught to be fearful that the planet would be destroyed in our lifetime unless we brought radical change to our Capitalist society. We "invented" recycling and drove VWs to save gas. Our brilliant textbooks posited that the way our planet could stave off destruction was through group action and political power.

The graduates of the 1970s are the "retirees" that are now leaving Fish and Game, the teaching profession at every level, the media, and the halls of state and national governmental agencies. They are the people that have held influence in our nation for the past forty years.

To accomplish both zero population and free love, birth control pills were enthusiastically recommended and provided free, courtesy of our government-sponsored health clinics! Abortion was widely believed to be of little more consequence than a haircut! Clinics were publicly funded everywhere! All was good! Love was free. Marriage commitment was old-fashioned and unnecessary. Boys could be boys forever because women could rule! The other method of controlling population mentioned openly in class was exploratory sex, which promised to fulfill the entire person. One of these explorations was homosexuality, the social benefit being it was all pleasure with no pregnancy.

Power to the People

The first time I had a teacher who actually discussed the social good of homosexuality in the classroom, I walked out to the beautiful day and sat on a bench, staring off to the glorious trees, manicured lawns, and stately building, but my mind was reeling. I had embraced TM, I had embraced ZPG, and I had embraced my biology professor's passion and mission to save the earth, save the whales, save the bald eagle, and save the redwoods. I was now trying to embrace this teaching that men were horrible, babies were a bad idea, and the dead White men who had written the moral standards of the past would have no effect on the present or on our future. I was beginning to question being part of this brave new world that would save the planet and give each of us self-realization. In the recesses of my mind, I felt like Alice running madly after the elusive Mad Hatter, in a land where nothing was as it seemed.

My Upper division classes were mostly education. Both the textbooks and the class material prepared well-meaning students graduating with good marks to enter the field of education fully able to indoctrinate young minds with the new world order but entirely unprepared to instruct in specific subject matter or the disciplines of logic and thought.

My university trained its teachers in social engineering, indoctrination, and psychology, and I suspect my university was not unique. They did not require teachers to be prepared with content-rich studies in geography, history, science, math, and literature. They did not teach methodology for class preparation to teach individual disciplines. There was a failure to give the student teachers an overview of where their piece of education would fit into the students' excellence of knowledge of history, math, reading, writing, and geography. The only area that was central for student teachers to impart to their students was concern for the environment. The focus on the environment in education would be the central theme around which a teacher could place the disciplines of writing, art, reading, etc. The education students were never challenged with learning logic and instructional methodology in such a way that it was a passion for them to teach subject matter.

Sadly, there was not a push for high academic standards and goals in the College of Education. The new college grading system meant that many classes were pass/fail, which encouraged mediocrity in our personal class performance. We were taught to be facilitators and classroom psychologists. We were taught to understand where the children were coming from and what obstacles they faced each day. The push to usher out the grading system of A–F in the school of education and replace it with pass/fail soon followed into the public school system. The purpose of eliminating grading was to build the students' self-esteem. Competition was discouraged because it was debilitating to some and supported a Capitalist economic format. The result of this grading change was the creation of a population of self-absorbed, mediocre people who were overconfident in their own abilities and lacked the wisdom humility instills. These college students of the seventies became the leaders of the nineties.

Hillary Clinton's commencement speech given at Wellesley College in 1969 is available to you with very little research. In the entire speech, I could find not a hint of gratitude for those who had gone before her graduating class. The introduction to her speech began with, "We're not in the positions yet of leadership and power, but we do have that indispensable task of criticizing and constructive protest." After outlining the gap between what is and what should be, Hillary again mentioned power, but this time she said, "Many of the issues that I've mentioned—those of sharing power and responsibility, those of assuming power and responsibilities—have been general concerns on campuses throughout the world."

The first portion of the speech criticized the current structure. The second point identified that those in power and responsibility were a concern to her. She outlined the reasonableness for protest and dissent and continued to offer no thanks or acknowledgment for the people that had provided the educational setting that she and her fellow students had enjoyed. She soon stated the goal of education (for her generation) was for "human liberation." They were to be the ones to liberate this nation from its current mores, current government, current economic policies, and current family structure.

Hillary made the assumption in her speech that her generation was the first to protest the status quo, that they were wiser than those who had gone before them and thus were given the responsibility of making things right. She intimated that the generation before was not trustworthy and had no integrity. She further intimated that they were not to be respected. She encouraged the new truth that they would create to become the guiding light for change. Truth would be defined by each individual, which would give total freedom. The attitude expressed was one that was superior to the current American citizen and the current American social structure. The desire to obtain the power to change the social structure fueled their passion. They were clear that the "old way" was wrong and that they could pioneer one true way—the new way would be the way of social justice. The classmates of Hillary are the national leaders of today.

The education curriculum to prepare teachers for the classroom was very different from the "teacher preparation" I have read about from the early part of the twentieth century. The discipline of students using memorization as a technique for instilling important documents was removed. The shared social values that once were the glue in public schools were removed with the Ten Commandments and the golden rule. The values of hard work, suffering, and thriftiness-will-pay-off-in-the-end were all removed. In place of systematic instruction in various disciplines, extra time was given to social organization of the child's mind in situational ethics exercises, or with the emphasis on environmental activism. When children march into school each day for twelve years of their lives and leave that public institution without substantial information regarding the history of their own nation or of Western civilization, they are unaware that throughout history man has struggled, had wars, experienced famine, and responded to leaders who demanded absolute power! They do not know that there are despots who have wielded absolute power while starving their own people. They are unaware that literally millions of citizens have been destroyed at the hand of their own national leadership. They are unaware that there have been climate changes throughout history, which are reflected in tree growth rings, rock formations, and much more.

These vastly uninformed young people with exalted impressions of their own knowledge make easy fodder for those who design to make them dependent pawns rather than independent citizens.

The state school system does not produce people who are informed about how the free enterprise market system works, which would allow them to succeed or fail on their own strength and merits. Nor are they shown, basic economics which instruct them on the freedoms of thrift and the prison created by debt. The classes on civics that were a part of the student's life in 1940s and 1950s and instructed students of the rights and responsibilities of American citizenship are gone. The current state school teaches that citizens have unlimited rights, which are obtained from a rich government, and the only responsibility is to save the planet!

For brevity's sake, suffice it to say that the basis of all teacher education was that a child is a blank slate. Whatever the society writes upon the slate, the child will embrace. There is no inherited spirituality, no core differentiation between boys and girls, no inherited mental strengths, no natural attraction for a girl child to play with dolls or a boy child to play with trucks—all children are the same. People are a material part of a material world. Another basic "truth" we future teachers learned was that children are intrinsically good and have great creative ability. The teacher was to be the facilitator and allow children to discover their full potential. The psychologist Jean Piaget was studied to understand the makeup of a child's development. The child's mind was able to move from one degree to another in a complexity of concepts. The use of rote memorization for specific information was not encouraged.

Think back to the college days and courses described. The education described took place in a university some thirty-seven years after the first *Humanist Manifesto* was written and the plan set into motion. The university exchanged the high goal of education to meet the goal of the master plan, which required the indoctrination of students for the future national change.

The educators of the seventies did not so much as attempt to instill a great passion for learning as they did instill a great passion for social involvement and social change. The educators of today assume that their classrooms are fully populated, secular humanist templates that have traveled the state school system. They expect to equip them to go into their social role with a secular humanist political view in order to move our country further to Socialism and, eventually, a one-world government. A modern student who does not fit the template will likely suffer at the hands of radical professors. A brief understanding of John Dewey reveals that he was a philosopher and chaired the Department of Philosophy in Chicago, but his deep interest was in education. His devotion to pedagogy led him to concrete beliefs regarding the school systems that were eventually put into practice throughout the state school systems. His key premise was that a school is a microcosm of society and that the process of education is a controlled version of the process of growth in the society. The classroom became more of a philosophical experiment in the 1960s rather than a place of instructing pupils in the facts of foundational subject matter. What we have today is the result of the classroom becoming a philosophical laboratory.

The rare students who retain a theist perspective of life and absolute values are treated as a classroom pariah. They are accosted with great rancor both from students and faculty. It appears the "mind" of the university has been made up and is now *closed* to any further discussion. One cannot help but think of Vice President Gore's proclamation regarding the issue of global warming: that the evidence is all in and there is nothing left to say about the matter. Since global warming is a matter of science, the material is voluminous and, in fact, not at all in agreement with itself. Science, by nature, is ever discovering new information, yet we are told that some topics are now closed—all the information is now in and may not have any challengers. These are any subjects that humanists must have control of in order to enslaved the population. Science is now in a box controlled by the humanist elites. To consider a medical procedure, a scientific study, or anything that is outside of their allowed parameters will be destroyed immediately through one or all their methods of control: the media, the entertainment industry, or the courts.

Whereas the college-educated student of the fifties was encouraged to be the best and brightest nurse, teacher, engineer, doctor, or theologian they could be, the 1970s college-educated person was instilled with tremendous guilt over the impact their humanity would bring on the planet. They were given projects that could alleviate the guilt for their humanity and make them become an effective part of the revolution. At every turn students were caught up in public protest and action. The College of Education did not so much as instill a desire to be the best teacher who turned out the brightest, highest-achieving students as they desired to turn out the most competent social change agents. The "good" teachers were impassioned to bring about the social change that they were being taught. They were to teach children the new religious view of environmental and social activism to bring about the new world order.

Essentially, we were useful idiots puffed up with the pride of the atheist revolution! Ironically, if the university was successful, we students would help to institute the intolerance of the system that our fathers and mothers had lost life and limb protecting Europe. It is no wonder that this plan has been so effectively and fervently moved forward, when we consider that the training has taken place within our most trusted public institution—the university.

The university students of today are being taught that the United States is destroying the planet because of its overuse of resources. They are taught that the economic system of free enterprise is unfair and opposes social justice. They are instilled with a set of citizen "rights" that include the right to food, clothing, shelter, education, and medical care. They are taught that Americans are racist and homophobic. They are instilled with the belief that all moral and ethical decisions are situational and to be made by them personally, not directed by the moral laws of a nonexistent God. These attitudes and beliefs perfectly align with the revolution.

After graduation, I learned five steps of the learning process which have been much more satisfying and have served well in assessing my personal grasp of subject material. I only wish that this simple understanding of the learning process had been taught in university as a preparation for teaching future students:

1. Level I: Rote Memorization—i.e., $2 + 2 = 4$.

2. Level II: Recognition—i.e., recognizing that $2 + 2$ always equals 4. There is a quick familiarity with the information. Think of it like a song that begins to play, and you begin to sing along because you recognize it but drop most of the lyrics because you don't quite know it—you "recognize" it.

3. Level III: Restatement—the ability to know the "fact" of $2 + 2 = 4$ so well that you are able to restate it and, in a sense, "teach" that fact to another.

4. Level IV: Relational—taking facts learned in one area of study and relating it to other facts to gain a fuller understanding (i.e., historical events, geographical information about a country, biographical information about the people in an era, and relating all to formulate an understanding about the time and society).

5. Level V: Revelational—this is a point of study where you have gathered and comprehended information from many different subjects and finally have that wonderful "Aha!" moment where you see and understand something. It can be spiritual, scientific, sociological, horticultural, artistic— whatever subject you have been attempting to grasp. It becomes yours, not just someone else's.

This type of systematic learning was anathema to the university system. The children were not to be given facts to memorize in order to gain information that would one day be able to be synthesized into their own well-reasoned understanding. The students, at any level, were to be treated as though their discovery of information made them superior. Thus, rather than teaching the system of phonics, the experimental "words in color," with charts and books and graphs, was instituted with great flair and hope. California ushered in "new math"—another great failure. And all the time the teachers were being taught to expect that teaching a student to read or to do math was an impossibly difficult task, and students and parents were learning that failure to learn was not related to teaching materials or methods but to social pressures on the student.

We went to college to be prepared to teach. We expected to become trained professionals. Many of us, like Hillary Rodham, got swept into a movement to become world changers. We came out believing we were classroom psychologists and designers of the next generation. The classroom became a setting where the materials and teaching practices were designed to serve the most debilitated student, which disallowed the average and above-average students to soar as they should. Our opinion of the teaching career was starkly different from that of the teacher who entered the classroom in 1930. We were to be the ones introducing these children

to the new ideas of society in the same way our wonderful professors had instructed us. The environment was everything, and personal fulfillment and pleasure a must. Ethics were to be personal and discovered by the child. Peace was to be achieved no matter the cost. Oil was bad, and oil companies worse. The government was to protect the individual citizen's liberty to achieve their own happiness.

It was during my college years that I learned that government provides the necessities. Many students lived off campus and availed themselves of food stamps, which were heretofore unknown to me. They expected public medical care at "clinics," public birth control again at the clinics. The "system" was there at our disposal to use and to enjoy. I worked two jobs and did not rely on the social system as provider.

As a junior, I was introduced to the world of economics. A remarkably bright spot in my education was discovered in an exceptional economics professor. The department was decidedly "conservative." Both of the professors that I studied under were proponents of free enterprise, and neither taught Keynesian economics as a good choice for a free nation. This was the first class that supported the values that were familiar to me upon entering university.

The economics department was unraveled, leaving only a few lower-division courses that fulfilled the liberal arts requirements. The major in economics was eliminated. I presumed that the building space and university budget were needed by the growing women's studies, African American studies, and Native American studies departments and their degrees. This substantial change in curriculum represents the changes being made in the citizen that was being shaped for the future of America.

So this was university in 1970–1974. The universities were working in concert for the hope and change that would yet take several generations to bring about. The students of the seventies finished their degrees, and those who would become the leaders of the nineties and to the current time went on to law school, on to Congress, into the governorships, and into politics at every level.

CHAPTER 4

Let's See the Blueprint

WWI was over, and the Great Depression was still taking its toll on American lives. It appeared that the spiritual life of the nation was at risk. While some came through the hard times stronger, many had their faith weakened. The elite had been awash in European thought, and Charles Darwin's influence was powerful in academia. The book *7 Men Who Rule the World from the Grave* by Dave Breese provides an excellent brief source on the background of seven men who greatly influenced the authors of the humanist blueprint for the revolution in America. These seven were Charles Darwin, Karl Marx, Julius Wellhausen, Sigmund Freud, John Dewey, John Maynard Keynes, and Søren Kierkegaard.

Darwin had died in 1882, and just a few years prior to Darwin's death,

Albert Einstein was born in 1872. Einstein's major scientific discoveries that would shape and shake the scientific communities took place in the 1930s. Some in the intellectual community began to believe that all of mankind's answers lay in science. The first *Humanist Manifesto* was born out of this intellectual environment. It first appeared in *The New Humanist* May/June 1933, volume 6, number 3.

The first "blueprint," as I have named them, is *Humanist Manifesto I*. It was written and set to work in 1933, expounded upon in 1967, and then clarified and strengthened in 2000 and 2003. *Manifesto I* and *Manifesto II* will be written in their entirety in the next several chapters, and we will consider the impact of each of the fifteen affirmations of *Manifesto I* and the seventeen affirmations in *Manifesto II*. The *2000 Manifesto* is very important but is book length, and so it will simply be referenced. The *2003 Manifesto* will also be referenced in this book.

Crucial to our understanding as we begin to study this document point by point is a brief mention of some of the signers on the document. Harry Elmer Barnes was generally regarded as the founding father of revisionist history and was a signer of the original manifesto. The first ever revisionist convention in 1979 was dedicated to Harry Barnes. Ernest Caldecott was a Unitarian minister who helped to validate humanist ideals in public schools. You may be familiar with his name because of the coveted Caldecott award given to authors of children's books. John Dewey, considered the father of modern education, was a primary author of this document. Dewey has been singularly responsible for the college preparation of public school teachers. Oliver L. Reiser was a professor at Pittsburg College and wrote the "credo of cosmic humanism." Roy Wood Sellars was a naturalist and philosopher who taught at the University of Michigan. He is the father of Wilfrid Sellars, who wrote extensively on atheism, activism, and pantheism. All the signers were influential, and many were in the field of education. In and of itself, the entire document, including introduction and signers, is four pages. There is an introduction followed by fifteen affirmations, which we will look at individually.

The *Humanist Manifesto II* was written in 1973, forty years after the first manifesto, and is a mere seven pages. *The Humanist Manifesto III* was published by the American Humanist Association in 2008 and is four pages. There is a great deal of writing from the humanists. Another crucial policy document is found in the book *Humanist Manifesto 2000: A Call for New Planetary Humanism* by Paul Kurtz. Taken together and comprehended, while seeming relatively minor because of brevity, these documents outline the beliefs and describe the changes expected within the new society. An important document has been submitted to Joe Biden to incorporate into his presidency. It is the twenty-eight-page document from the Secular Democrats of America entitled "Restoring Constitutional Secularism and Patriotic Pluralism in the White House." It is an important look both at what President Trump did to broaden religious rights and the direction the humanists are requesting of Joe Biden.

It is remarkable, but true, that to understand these documents is to understand the quiet revolution that has taken place in America over the past eighty-seven years. These documents explain why we have a citizenry who is divided and why they vote the way they do. It explains national activism in both political and social programs. To understand these documents is to understand where you, the reader, are on the continuum of transformation from traditional Judeo-Christian-based beliefs to atheistic humanism. My goal is to shed a bright light on the confusion that is the Two Americas.

The introduction to *Humanist Manifesto I* is very instructive. It accomplishes the following points:

1. Establishes the need for social change.

2. Defines the new state religion which will be instituted.

3. Enumerates the change required and the actions that must be taken.

4. Introduces the new religion, which is designed to replace the outmoded one. More importantly, it replaces what they believe to be a religion "dangerous" to society and the individual with

something that they perceive as "good" for them.

5. Brings sufficient social goals and personal satisfactions to adequately meet the needs of citizens. The humanists believe in "doing good without God."

6. Teaches that individuals must adhere to the beliefs and principles set within the various manifestos, resulting in a move away from the individual and toward community good. There would be a social structure with one mind and one spirit. (Goebbels comes to mind once again.)

The introduction to *Humanist Manifesto I*, in part, follows:

> The time has come for widespread recognition of the radical changes in religious beliefs throughout the modern world. The time is past for mere revision of traditional attitudes. Science and economic change have disrupted the old beliefs. Religions the world over are under the necessity of coming to terms with new conditions created by a vastly increased knowledge and experience. In every field of human activity, the vital movement is now in the direction of the candid and explicit humanism. In order that religious humanism[1] may be better understood we, the undersigned, desire to make certain affirmations which we believe the facts of our contemporary life demonstrates.

> There is great danger of a final, and we believe fatal, identification of the word religion with doctrines and methods which have lost their significance and which are powerless to solve the problem of human living in the Twentieth Century. Religions have always been means

---

[1] Such a vital, fearless, and frank religion capable of furnishing adequate social goals and personal satisfaction may appear to many people as a complete break with the past.

for realizing the highest values of life.[2] Their end has been accomplished through the interpretation of the total environing situation (theology or world view) established for realizing the satisfactory life. A change in any of these factors results in alteration of the outward forms of religion.

This fact explains the changefulness of religions through the centuries, but through all changes religion itself remains constant in its quest for abiding values, an inseparable feature of human life. [This is copied exactly from the manifesto.]

Today, man's larger understanding of the universe, his scientific achievements, and his deeper appreciation of brotherhood have created a situation that requires a new statement of the means and purposes of religion. While this age does owe a vast debt to traditional religions, it is nonetheless obvious that any religion that can hope to be a synthesizing and dynamic force for today must be shaped for the needs of this age. It is a responsibility that rests upon this generation. We therefore affirm the following.

This introduction makes one thing vitally clear: the manifesto that we are about to engage is one of a new religion to replace all old, outdated religions. It is recognized here that up to this point, America's social goals, personal satisfaction, and means for realizing the highest values of life have been found in the citizen's relation to their religions. The religions that are referenced are generally the various sects of Christianity and Judaism.

The first and most emphatic fact upon which every other doctrine in the *Humanist Manifesto* rests is that God does not exist and as such there must be a grand exchange. Everything that is based on the belief in the

---

2   To establish such a religion is a major necessity of the present.

Judeo-Christian God must be exchanged for an atheistic belief system.

There have been a number of court cases, some reaching the Supreme Court, regarding the religious standing of secular humanism. Several very complicated cases have been fought to determine if humanism is actually a religion in and of itself. Torcaso v. Watkins is a case frequently cited. It is a complex case and finding, but I quote a brief portion of the conclusion below:

> In *Torcaso v. Watkins* 367 U.S. 488 (1961), decided at the Supreme Court, Roy Torcaso was refused an office of Notary Public because he would not declare his belief in God, as required by Maryland Constitution. Claiming this violated the 1st and 14th Amendments, he sued the state. He claimed it violated his right to religion. It was held that the test for public office could not be enforced because it *invaded his freedom of belief and religion* [italics mine] provided in the 1st amendment, and protected by the 14th amendment.

While this does not specifically establish humanism, or atheism, as a religion, the context of their own documents refers to humanism as a religion, that it is their "replacement religion" for theistic religions.

One paragraph in the Torcaso case findings is particularly interesting, so it is included below:

> The "establishment of religion" clause of the First Amendment means at least this: neither a state nor the Federal Government can set up a church. Neither can pass laws *which aid one religion, aid all religions, or prefer one religion over another* [italics mine]. Neither can force nor influence a person *to go to or to remain* [italics mine] away from church against his will or force him to *profess a belief or disbelief in any religion* [italics mine]. No person can be punished for entertaining or professing religious beliefs or

disbeliefs, for church attendance or nonattendance. No tax in any amount, large or small, can be levied to support any religious activities or institutions, whatever they may be called, or whatever form they may adopt to teach or practice religion. Neither a state nor the Federal Government can, openly or secretly, participate in the affairs of any religious organizations or groups, and vice versa. In the words of Jefferson, the clause against establishment of religion by law was intended to erect "a wall of separation between church and State."

If secular humanism is a religion, as they state in their introduction to *Humanist Manifesto I*, it may follow that neither the state nor the federal government would be allowed to set up or establish that church in any public institution to the exclusion of all other religions.

This "wall of separation" was inappropriately adopted from a document Jefferson wrote that had the intention of protecting the church from the influence of the state, not the other way around!

For a fully documented case study of the separation of church and state, I recommend my readers search the pages of *The Myth of Separation* by David Barton.

For the secular humanists to accomplish the full exchange from our theistic culture to a fully humanist atheistic one, the humanists would need to overturn and rewrite law. They would need to overcome such staunch findings as cited in *Church of the Holy Trinity v. United States*. In this 1992 Supreme Court decision, the court cited no less than forty-four state constitutions and utilized a broad and convincing argument where they concluded that the United States is a Christian nation (cited from David Barton's *The Myth of Separation*).

LINDA NELSON

The First Affirmation in the *Humanist Manifesto I*

Religious humanists regard the universe as self-existing and not created.

All material that is a quote of the Humanist documents will be copied as printed with any intrinsic errors standing. Let us consider, in brief, the effects that this affirmation has made on the public education system. There has been a concerted effort using the force of the courts via repeated lawsuits (primarily through the ACLU and similar legal groups) to remove every mention and tradition of God from all public education; all social traditions of Christmas, Easter, religious plays, music, and festivities have come under such a continual barrage of attack that school administrators will scarcely let "Silent Night" be sung! Winter holiday and spring break have been instituted to replace the familiar Christmas and Easter vacations of our childhood. The spirituals we sang as children when learning the history of the South and how the slaves coped with their terrible conditions, their suffering, and their resilience are banned. The music that formed a common thread in my childhood to other members of our society has been removed. Speakers who earn the right as valedictorian to address their classmates are forbidden to give thanks to the God whom they love and serve.

Legal battles have removed nativity scenes and crosses from public lands, and there have been attempts to remove them from private property as well.

With the removal of God, all absolute authority has been removed from the public school. One cannot posit that God is Creator in the public school setting without a legal backlash. The Ten Commandments as moral directives have been removed from all public schools, courthouses, and other public properties. Parents and teachers in the past were afforded honor and the ability to exercise absolute authority as an extension of God's absolute authority. It goes without saying, however, that some exercised their authority well, with kindness and measure, and some badly. This moral base, reflecting the authority of position, has been replaced with teachers as facilitators and students as omnipotent rulers over their own destiny. Students are taught to establish their own personal morality and ethics based on the situation at hand and not to consider absolutes that establish principled decision-making. In short, the foundations are removed. No longer can you teach young people to defer sexual intimacy until marriage; they learn that they are the arbiter of their own truth in this area and are to do whatever they believe they want to do when they are ready.

All school literature has been stripped of God, prayer, and faith. Textbook publishers edit illustrations to make certain of equal representation of ethnicity and gender and carefully remove any pictures or references to God, Jesus, or Christianity.

American children are no longer taught common principles of citizenship based on commonly held biblical principles and common moral codes in their public education. They are now given basic character qualities, such as truthfulness and kindness and justice, that they are encouraged to incorporate in their moral framework. The belief that there is a god or that they will ultimately be accountable for their own lives is completely removed.

The early public school systems used *The New England Primer*, the McGuffey Readers, and the family Bibles as their reading texts. Each was replete with moral instruction for living and references to Providence and the Creator. This is all gone, and as we will see, a "new morality" and a new religion have replaced the old.

The complete removal of prayer from every public meeting and classroom has been demanded. This is not only contrary to our history but is also contrary to our Senate, which still opens with daily prayer!

The instruction of evolution at all levels as scientific fact, presented without a possible alternative, is a closely held treasure of the humanists.

The outcome of the Scopes trial was the beginning of many trials to follow and undoubtedly encouraged the authors of the first manifesto that the time had come to replace the antiquated belief system with one based upon religious humanism.

Evolution is the lynchpin to all other thoughts and affirmations. It remains the absolute foundational principle that affirms the humanist's first principle, which asserts that "there is no God." It is defended in courts, in the media, in entertainment, and in the school system. Humanists go to great lengths to keep scientists who are proponents of intelligent design away from the positions that would allow them to speak authoritatively regarding their views on intelligent design. Exemplified in the documentary *Expelled* by Ben Stein.

The effect of this first affirmation on public institutions was much like its effect on education. The use of the courts to enforce the blanket removal of God from those institutions has been the same. Test cases are carefully chosen by the ACLU et al. in every public arena where a cross, nativity scene, scripture, prayer, or the Bible can be discovered. Wherever is found a person who may be offended by a hint of God, the ACLU gladly embraces the opportunity to sue and continue in the secularization of American culture.

The removal of God from education has necessitated the removal of the Founders' principles and code of ethics. The radical changes in American history and culture have been a great frustration for the Americans who hold to the Founders' view of the Constitution, while the secular humanist citizen is thoroughly delighted. The disappearance of the fact of God, who is Creator, from our culture has taken much longer than the humanists had expected, but we stand on the very brink of that change being complete in America today. One wonders if every American who was a theist and supported our founding documents stood up and shouted "Stop!" if it would be possible to retrieve what is left of our godly heritage. There are some working very hard to preserve that heritage, and they would say without a doubt, "Yes."

Religion and Society

If one desired to do a brief study of the sovereign nations of the world and attempt to define the differences in culture, one would certainly examine their economic system and the commodities that they can buy and sell. One would consider their education and health systems, their languages and income, but first and foremost, one would consider their spiritual makeup. The spiritual condition of a nation is a driving force behind wealth, education, health, economics, and every other area of both public and private life.

As our nation has begun its decline in the social fabric, there are deleterious effects of national strength of our country. This weakening of the most powerful nation on earth is required if a one-world government is to be put into place.

If we considered, Iraq we could not help but realize that their faith is the primary motivator of international relations. The divide between the Shia and Sunni sects of the Muslim faith has provided fodder for war that dates back to the death of the prophet Muhammad in AD 632.

The spiritual heritage of a nation is foundational to all other factors in the nation. I have been interested to hear American news commentators push for a "secular" Israel and "secular" Egypt. The Arab Spring in the Middle East in 2012 was discussed with great hope by our American media because, while they were clear that the Muslim brotherhood could be the next controlling interest in Egypt or Libya, the American commentators believed that the Muslim brotherhood would act as secular humanists once they were in power. From the perspective of a media who has worked diligently to remove the Christian influence from America, it is clear that they are not concerned about a Muslim influence because they have convinced themselves that the "brotherhood" will lead a "secular state." The secular humanist, American education system is also welcoming to Muslim religious teachings, as evidenced by Muslim curricula that have been instituted in some states. The Council on American-Islamic Relations, or CAIR, has been working with textbook publishers and the

American Teachers Association to produce textbooks and curriculum for Islamic studies. Brigitte Gabriel has actively uncovered the move to include detailed Islamic religious studies in the public schools while they cleanse the public schools of the God of our Judeo-Christian heritage.

Ms. Gabriel has documented a course taught in California seventh-grade public school children. The course is called "A Course on Islam." The schoolchildren are to become Muslim for three weeks. They dress and eat as Muslims. They choose Islamic names, they are to memorize wisdom cards from the Koran, and before the end of the course, they will visit a mosque.

One of the wisdom cards instructs the student on how to become a Muslim and the prayer that they must say. Another wisdom card that is memorized by the students deals with the definition of *jihad*. They will memorize that "a jihad is a struggle by Muslims against oppression, invasion, and injustice." These are the talking points of the radical Muslims!

The students are taught the following prayer and then lead in analyzing it and saying it:

> Ash-hadu alla ilaha illallah-wa ash-hadu anna
> Muhammadan abduhu wa rasulullah.

> I bear witness that there is no God except Allah and
> Muhammad [was] is His messenger.

One cannot, in one's wildest dreams, imagine that the Christian prayer acknowledging individual sin and accepting God's forgiveness through the sacrifice of Jesus Christ as Lord and Savior could become part of a three-week public school curriculum; but for some reason, there is no conflict between Islam and secular humanists when considering curriculum for the public school system. Perhaps it could be that the humanist goal is to transform American history and culture; hence, the Muslim religion and customs do not present a threat to it. Each nation does have a spiritual heritage, and ours is not Islam, nor is it atheism. We have a rich heritage of personal faith in the God of the Bible. Many also believe in Jesus Christ, who they believe to be one of the triune God revealed in the Bible. This rich heritage is well-woven through early literature, early court documents, monuments, and educational materials, such as *The New England Primer*, widely used in our early schools, as well as the Geneva Bible. Because we have a Judeo-Christian social framework, our national work ethic, our family structure, our economic structure, and our legal structure are all aligned with our moral base. In order to form a secular nation, each of these structures must be systematically stripped away and new ones instituted to form a new moral conscience and public practice. This is the aim of those who would move us to a secular society. The current exchange of culture and religion from a Judeo-Christian-based society to a secular state regards the state as the final authority in the lives of individuals. The individual is submitted to the state and to the collective will.

The United States' Judeo-Christian-based culture has deep beliefs of tolerance, love, and the exercise of free will with regard to religious beliefs. Hence, the First Amendment grants freedom of religion and speech equality to all. Because our very laws, nature, and beliefs allowed us to be systematically silenced and tolerant toward others, our culture was putty in the hands of the secular humanist revolutionaries. When Christians opposed the cultural changes, such as removal of prayer from public schools, they were labeled bigots, intolerant, judgmental, and hateful. These accusatory words were used in my college classes to describe those who opposed sex education for elementary school children, abortion for minors without parental consent, or those who failed to embrace open marriage, living together out of wedlock, and homosexuality. These words would still be used for those who hold these beliefs today.

Genuinely caring Christians took to heart the accusations, searched their minds and consciences for ill feelings, and began to bow to the intolerant secular demands for dominance. At the core of the onslaught, let us be clear: the Judeo-Christian culture was not attempting to foist their beliefs into and onto the culture. They were the base from which the culture had blossomed.

The Christian belief structure and acknowledgment of God's creation and authority were noted in the Mayflower Compact, in nearly all the early documents, both state and national, by which governmental authority was established.

The acknowledgment of a Creator God was the foundational fact from which law and social structure emerged. The very covenant form of government assuring the citizens that their rights could not be severed from them was in the fact that God had given these rights. Further, it was this covenant form of government that limited the government's power, scope, and reach over the citizen; every area of government was to be limited in scope and reach.

For the first affirmation of the *Humanist Manifesto* to be enacted, it would require that God would be abandoned in the public square, as well as in the heart of the individual citizen. Our law, our government, our personal lives, our medical systems, our military and educational systems must all be stripped of God. While abandonment in the belief of God individually as citizens may be slow to come, the elimination of God from practice in culture, work, and education would soon breed a generation free of the limits of a prayer hearing God. The implementation of this plan would begin with education and utilize the media to capture public opinion. It would then codify into law the new practices, thus institutionalizing humanism. With these things in place, the secular revolution would be accomplished. Since this was in direct opposition to the foundations of our government, the government must be changed from the bottom up and top down until one day the documents could be changed to reflect the new culture! We now stand on the brink of such a moment. Listen to the chatter and you will hear the desire for a constitutional convention to change our documents, which would formally complete the revolution and the end to the covenant.

The Second Affirmation in the *Humanist Manifesto I*

Humanism believes that man is a part of nature and that he has emerged as a result of a continuous process.

This affirmation serves as an instruction on educational change.

The humanist must exchange the Creator God for evolution. Evolution must be absolutely authoritative but considered proven fact. It is this affirmation that demands that the theory of evolution be treated as a scientific fact. This educational principle would dictate funding, textbooks, hiring of educators, and the award of academic honors from 1933 until today. It would place evolutionists and environmentalists as the dictators of all actions regarding the public purse strings in funding of projects, public policies, and national education.

Consider now the university that I described in the early pages of this book. It is clear that there was a purpose to the university's instruction and indoctrination. The college, to be aligned with the new humanist world order, could only accept and consider one point of view regarding man's beginnings and the impact of humans on the environment. To approach the subject of biology from an environmental alarmist point of view at the college level meant that we, as teachers, would indoctrinate an environmental alarmist point of view to our students once we entered our profession in the public schools.

The university became the arbitrators of future generations via a specific indoctrination of young men and women prior to their childbearing years. This indoctrination discouraged childbearing for the sake of the planet. If the student embraced the indoctrination, one would commit to having no more children than to replace oneself. The only moral position a couple could have would be to limit their family to two children.

The university education that we looked at earlier made an exchange of the systematic study of factual subject matter with a course of study that openly indoctrinated the student to a "sustainable planet" mindset.

These new courses used books such as Carson's *Silent Spring* and Ehrlich's *Population Bomb* by way of presenting an undisputed scientific fact. These are now very old books, but their ideas are still at work in the minds of many people. As we all can see, the year 2020 has not borne out their terror. We are still here as a planet and doing well in many ways. Today's classroom has a strong emphasis on global warming, and we have alarmists saying it is the most crucial issue of our time. Their warning is that we only have ten years before it's too late. This is patterned after the scare tactics of 1965. *Climategate*, written by Brian Sussman, a veteran meteorologist, is ignored as a balancing argument as are other noted scientists.

The Third Affirmation in the *Humanist Manifesto I*

Holding an organic view of life, humanists find that the traditional dualism of mind and body must be rejected.

This concept exposes humanist "truth" that all is material or organic and nothing is created. The concept is rooted in Marxism, and with this we see many crossovers to the Marxist thinking. The Judeo-Christian view of life holds the concept of a triune man: a body, soul, and spirit. The soul representing man's mind, will, and emotions; the body his flesh and its nature; and the spirit, which is touched by God's Spirit. In the Judeo-Christian perspective, the body suffers earthly temptations, sickness and joy, and finally, death, but the spirit and soul remain and are eternal. The Judeo-Christian founding philosophies would address body, soul, and spirit in an educational system. The memorization and recitation of scripture was commonplace in early American education. The mind was developed in such a way as to grasp the consequence of behavior which contradicts God's moral directives. The desires of the body were kept under discipline to the spirit and the mind. The overall goal was to live a good life in respect to God and others, with the certain expectation that the life you live will be examined by God in the end.

The humanist can misrepresent, lie, and manipulate facts, and even publicly destroy other people, in order to obtain their desired end. This can be entirely without conscience because all is material; there is no spirit and no soul. This is consistent with a humanist worldview. We should not be surprised when we see that in the Josephson Institute Survey of Teens, completed in 2000, seven out of ten admitted to cheating on a test at least once in the last year and nearly half said they had done so more than once. It further found in the Report Card on the Ethics of American Youth that 92 percent of the 8,600 students lied to their parents in the past year and 78 percent lied to their teachers. More than one in four said they would lie to get a job. One in four has shown up for class drunk at least once in the past year, and 68 percent have admitted hitting someone because they were angry at them.

One may conclude that most of these teens think that they are happy with their personal ethics. Could this be because they are schooled in developing their own set of ethics and they are rarely presented with the nature of a holy God? The student believes that their personal standard need not be based on an absolute standard such as the Ten Commandments?

Should this revolution be completed, the ultimate authorities in the citizens' lives will be governmental agencies. The key feature of the religious humanist is that they believe that they are producing a citizen who will do good without God. The humanist believes the concept of sin, and therefore salvation, to be harmful because to sin is to "miss the mark of God's will." That is to say, if there is no God, there is obviously no one's will that exceeds the individual's! In the humanist ethical system, perfect harmony is to be found doing what you want to do. To be part of a group of activists working in concert to bring about change is nirvana. To be "good" in their own eyes, they are doing well in their field of social influence. Their action is in some way redemptive; it gives them personal approval and stature in the eyes of their peers. Ironically, the true humanist can march for world peace while being at war with their life partner or the father or mother of their children. The peace they march for in the streets may elude them in their personal lives without any recognition of the inconsistency. It is also consistent with their ethical perspective to decry the brutality of the police while simultaneously brutally destroying the homes, businesses, property, and lives of other people. They remain "good in their own eyes" as long as they are fighting for what they believe is an ethical outcome.

Maintaining lifelong, peaceful, permanent relationships with another person for the goal of rearing children in a cohesive setting was at the core of the Founders' character requirements. Divorce was difficult to obtain, and irresponsibility for children was so much abhorred that social pressure of "doing what is right" often kept families together and husbands home and providing for their children.

To maintain the Founders' principles requires a personal awareness that life is more than material. The acknowledgment of soul and spirit in the human nature then demands an education system that appeals to conscience and responsibility to God.

The current religion of humanism, as taught in the state school system, demands sex education from a purely material perspective. Humanism requires that sex education provide full information as early as possible, regarding methods of contraception, sexual disease, and abortion. They attempt to teach by way of defining all forms of sexual activity as legitimate. They currently encourage discussion on gender choice. They provide information on whom to speak to regarding supplies and where to turn in case of a pregnancy. They provide no training regarding what age sex should be entered into. The main focus of the discussion is to encourage protection against unwanted pregnancy and disease, and information about how to terminate an unwanted pregnancy should one occur. This education would be consistent with their philosophy, which rejects the traditional Judeo-Christian belief in body, soul, and spirit.

In stark contrast, the Founders' education surrounding this topic would require an entirely different approach. A traditional class would include the biology of pregnancy and childbirth, but it would be taught in the context of lifelong parental commitments. A class designed around a traditional point of view may instruct teenaged children that their teen years and early adult years are the years they develop talents, strengths, and then an understanding of how to apply those talents and strengths to have a life that is full and worth living. The instruction would help these young people see how these strengths may also be used in industry or business so they begin to focus on the responsibilities life will bring. It may contain information about health and safety of a home, the needs of children at all levels, the nutrition requirements for healthy children, and healthy lifestyles. The course would necessitate the instruction on disease, on character qualities you might find in a life mate, on financial matters of running a home. Thus, traditional family life education would reflect the family in its entirety. It would incorporate sexuality into the family unit, where children are raised up for the next generation. It would be taught with the traditional view of one man / one woman for life. This would reinstate the family unit as the nation's foundation. The result would be strong families and a stronger nation.

The home could add specific doctrine held by the family to this education but would not find that the school was either demeaning or countering their family's tightly held beliefs.

The outcome of our state school systems' humanist sex education program is that we now have a "hookup" generation, oftentimes devoid of tenderness and commitment. The school system's education has been reinforced by our humanist media and entertainment. The result of the past thirty years of public instruction appears to have left many young people hungry for deep, lasting relationships. Many habitually float from one relationship to another, with no permanent commitment. The sex education programs are some of the major influences to teach children that they are purely material beings.

It may be argued that the indoctrination of the material nature of man apart from soul and spirit, and the accompanying eternality promised in our Founders' philosophy, could be complicit in escalating school violence due to the dehumanization of the individual. A traditional thinker may also argue that we may be better equipped to turn this culture of violence around by nurturing the child's spirit and soul.

Benjamin Rush, a signer of the Declaration of Independence, who ratified the Constitution and served in the administrations of John Adams and Thomas Jefferson, had this to say about violence in public schools:

In contemplating the political institutions of the United States, if we remove the Bible from schools I lament that we waste so much time and money in punishing crimes and take so little pains to prevent them.

Another basic change that the humanists are insisting on is the removal of guns from the hands of the individual citizen. The traditional citizen knows that the retention of the Second Amendment is crucial to retaining all the other rights that have been promised in the Constitution.

It is helpful to ask why some of the mass shootings have occurred. What has precipitated that helped to form a person wholly devoid of conscience? Can we consider that the type of bloody, nonsensical violence we have seen in school, church, and nightclub shootings has at its roots an atheist view of life rather than a theist view of life? Is violence of this nature an expected outcome of the numbing of our spiritual nature? The humanist premise that all people are material beings with no soul and no spirit, that we are purely material in nature, defies everything a child feels from the time they are born and seek comfort and love. This humanist philosophy encourages individuals to be focused on their individual "rights" rather than "responsibilities."

When one views the world from the seat of a "victim," it may not be as hard to exercise bitter anger against a competitor. A Judeo-Christian outlook on life that was previously held by our citizens would simply state, "The rain falls on the just and the unjust." Under our Founders' system, fairness is not expected in life, but there is a certain expectation that all men will face trials which, when persevered through, will produce godly character.

The newest evidence of this affirmation that is being seen in our state school system is gender confusion. Since the humanist system does not acknowledge the soul or spirit of mankind, it would be contrary to this affirmation to acknowledge the differentiation in the creation of God. The current humanist system, through state schools, will encourage gender confusion in our youngest children. The push for homosexuality, transgender, and other gender "options" is a logical next step in the transformation to a purely secularized society.

The Fourth Affirmation in the *Humanist Manifesto I*

Humanism recognizes that man's religious culture and civilization, as clearly depicted by anthropology and history, is the product of a gradual development due to his interaction with his natural environment and with his social heritage. The individual born into a particular culture is largely molded to that culture.

This affirmation not only establishes the goal of eliminating the religious base of our nation but also describes how they will replace it with the new religion of humanism. If they are to accomplish the exchange of traditional religion with the new and better religion of humanism, they must do so by molding the minds of individuals from as early an age as possible (as seen in the statement "The individual born into"). It has taken multiple generations, but through time and coordination of effort, the exchange is very far along. The humanists concentrate on the young and develop their worldview gradually in the laboratory of the state school system. This explains the push for earlier childhood education so that secular humanism can become the belief system of the nearly infant child.

The natural environment, interaction in all public places, and social change will eventually create a national atmosphere wherein all citizens will be homogeneously humanists. Let's consider how this happens: Workplaces that demand that their employees not wear a cross necklace but can walk in gay parades in the work aprons. Think Home Depot. A workplace that does not allow a Christian screensaver on a computer (a large local automobile distributer). An employee fired because of wearing a "Jesus loves you" pin. A homeowner sued for having a crèche on their lawn, a church sued for having a crèche on their lawn, and a church prohibited from having a live crèche at Christmas. The individual stories could fill a book, but there is no doubt that the workplace has been reshaped to fit into the humanist social structure.

Public education used to reflect the dependence of our Founding Fathers' both on God and on His mercy. The acknowledgment of God was woven into the fabric of a child's education and our social interaction. The school system did not teach a religion; however, the public schools reflected Judeo-Christian thought as a philosophy of life and as a moral structure for the public school culture. They did not teach specific doctrines of a specific religion, yet they taught and instilled a theist worldview. The public schools reflected a public theistic point of view and acknowledged both God and Jesus but did not add the doctrine of specific sects. Today it represents unwaveringly an atheistic point of view that is intolerant to all other thought. Christianity, while probably having the greatest representation of theists in our population, has an amazing number of separate "sects" within that theological persuasion. Each sect has distinct interpretations of Scripture and practice. These Christian sects have experienced some disagreement between one another, such as Catholic versus Protestant or even strict Calvinists versus Armenian thinkers. To teach a specific church's doctrine, such as was done with the Church of England in Britain, would violate the intent and the letter of the First Amendment. The public school system prior to 1940 had a relatively uniform recognition of God, and pictures of Jesus, plaques of the Ten Commandments, and other religious symbols were regularly found in the public school. Regular prayer was part of the opening school day for a schoolchild. The twenty-two-word prayer that was spoken by schoolchildren at the time the ACLU brought suit to stop prayer in the state schools is as follows:

Almighty God, we acknowledge our dependence upon
Thee, and we beg Thy blessings upon us, our parents and
our teachers and our Country.

This general, nondenominational prayer did not establish a specific religion, such as Lutheran or Catholic with all their attending doctrine, but was general and agreeable to all theists. It asked God to bless our nation, our school, and our families. This small prayer fit a theist point of view apart from any specific religious indoctrination. In order to accomplish the fourth affirmation, the humanists knew that every vestige of a reference to God must be eliminated. The victory in the lawsuit *Engel v. Vitale* went a

Sexually Transmitted Diseases
Gonorrhea
Age Group: 10–14

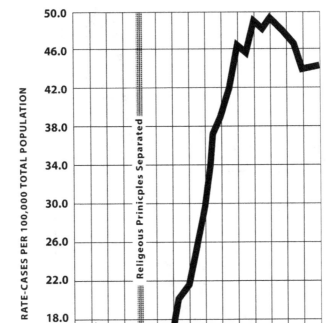

Basic data from the Center for Disease Control
and the Department of Health and Human Services

Sexually Transmitted Diseases
Ages 15–19

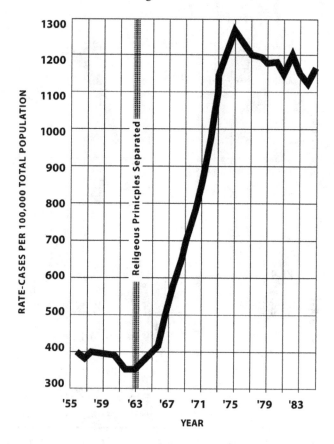

Basic data from the Center for Disease Control
and the Department of Health and Human Resources

Pregnancy to Unwed Girls Under 15 Years of Age

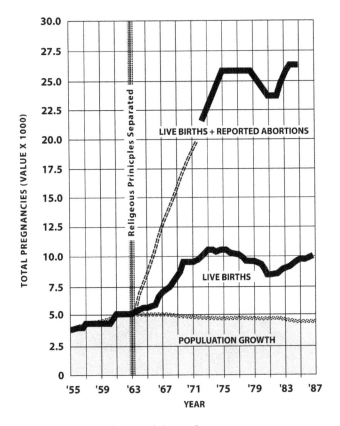

Basic data from the Department of Health and Human Services

Pregnancy for Unwed Girls 15–19 Years of Age

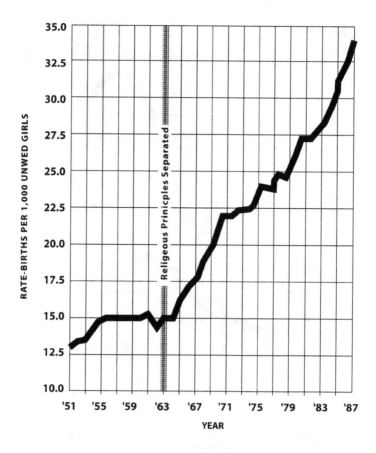

Basic data from the Department of Health and Human Services

very long way in the direction of moving God out of our public education. Upon removing this general prayer from the schools, it effectively stripped away a theist perspective and established an intolerant religion of atheism. At the same time that God was ushered out of the public school, the Constitution was compromised, along with all our unabashed Christian history. The revisionists went to work to strip the mention of God out of textbooks. The God that was recognized readily in our early documents and was mentioned on all our state and federal buildings and was sought every day as Congress opened was now removed from public schools.

In its place was not just a void but a new religion of atheism. Once the religion of atheism was established in the state-controlled and statefunded education system, its power and influence were effectively in every child's life. The drastic step of removing God and prayer from the state's school has produced dire consequences. I have included below a few graphs that aid in having a picture of the results, but the full impact of the removal of God's name and blessing on the children, their parents, their teachers, and their country may be seen in the book *America: To Pray or Not to Pray* by David Barton.

The state schools further conformed the student to the new humanist mold by stripping godly character qualities from the curriculum. Humility, gentleness, patience, faithfulness, and godliness are all gone. Prior to the removal of prayer, authority was absolute and God-given. Children were a reflection of their family and taught to honor the family name. While public school had a general agreement that God existed, no specific religious doctrine was taught.

The following graphs indicate the changes that occurred to the young population when prayer was removed from public schools.

Individuals were allowed to bring their personal traditions and teachings from their home to interpret who God was and what He required of them. The public school and public forums were an eclectic place of many ideas, tolerant to each and most decidedly theistic. As previously mentioned, the Ten Commandments lent a moral framework, as did the golden rule of "Do unto others as you would have them do unto you." This place of religious presence in the classroom was completely in keeping with the founding documents, institutions, and practices. There was no intolerance of the child's thoughts. If a child came from an atheist home, they had full voice in the classroom, with no coercion to conform and the right to opt out of any exercise that would offend their sensibilities. All children coming from theist homes shared in certain common, broad beliefs that created cohesion among students and provided social boundaries. The body, soul, and spirit were recognized by children and teachers. They were taught not to violate their conscience with unseemly language or behavior.

Of course, the students were not pure as the driven snow; they were flawed, as people are. They did, however, share a common behavioral heritage and an honor of God the Creator.

Because we have been focusing on education, I believe it is pertinent to take a small detour to look at a few documents that will give a very good understanding of the change in educational principles.

The US Constitution makes no mention of the purpose or function of public schools. The responsibility of education was directed historically from the individual communities, and many state constitutions address public education. The local control of education took another huge leap into the revolution of a one-world government as the federal government took greater control of education through the Common Core agenda. This program was tantamount to the federal government mandating every aspect of education, from early childhood through college; all states were to adopt the curricula and the testing methods. As I write this book, we are now in the midst of the virus that has unleashed change to our nation which we cannot yet measure. We do not know what schools, businesses, money, church, and parties will all look like going forward.

Long term, it has the potential of granting more federal control over every action of the citizen's life. I mention this here because we do not know what school will look like in the future, but we may safely guess that for the secular humanist it will look more nearly like the secularist twenty-first century prophesied those many years ago.

The most comprehensive view of the purpose of education is given by John Adams in postcolonial Massachusetts as follows:

> Wisdom, and knowledge, as well as virtue, diffused
> generally among the body of the people, being necessary
> for the preservation of their rights and liberties; and as these
> depend on spreading the opportunities and advantages of
> education in the various parts of the country, and among
> the different orders of the people, it shall be the duty of

legislatures and magistrates, in all future periods of this commonwealth, to cherish the interests of literature and the sciences, and all seminaries of them; especially the university at Cambridge, public schools and grammar schools in the towns; to encourage private societies and public institutions, rewards and immunities, for the promotion of agriculture, arts, sciences, commerce, trades, manufactures, and a natural history of the country; to countenance and inculcate the principles of humanity and general benevolence, public and private charity, industry and frugality, honesty and punctuality in their dealings; sincerity, good humor, and all social affections and generous sentiments among the people. [Commonwealth of Massachusetts]

In "Using School Mission Statements for Reflection and Research" by Steven E. Stemler, Damian Bebell, and Lauren Ann Sonnabend, they note the following:

John Dewey in 1938 argued that: "the primary purpose of education and schooling is not so much to prepare students to live a useful life but to teach them how to live pragmatically and immediately in the context of their current environment." In contrast George Counts (1978), a leading progressive educator in the 1930's, critiqued Dewey's philosophy, stating, "the weakness of progressive education thus lies in the fact that it has elaborated no theory of social welfare, unless it be that of anarchy or extreme individualism." ...Counts emphasized that the primary purpose of school is "preparation for social integration and social reconstruction."

This statement by John Dewey is the purest form of the humanist state dream.

By contrast, let me copy below three current school statements. One taken from my home city, Tucson's Unified School District; one from Elgin School District (a small rural Arizona school), and one from Hillsdale College (a private university that more nearly reflects the Founders' values).

You will find that by contrast both the Elgin Unified School and the Tucson Unified School district are completely void of the characteristics you will see in the Hillsdale College Statement.

Tucson Unified School District
Tucson Unified School District Organizational Values

- We value classrooms as the core of successful education.

- We value diversity through intercultural proficiency.

- We value each student as an individual who will learn.

- We value teamwork among students, parents, colleagues, and the community to achieve common goals.

- We value collective inquiry to find new methodologies for success.

- We value and celebrate positive results, taking pride in our efforts that produce them.

- We value exceptional service to students, parents/guardians, colleagues, and community.

*****

Elgin School (A K-8)

Elgin School is a safe and caring learning community committed to the development of the whole child. Our mission is to engage all children in the art and work of childhood, to provide them a solid academic foundation, and to have them demonstrate responsible citizenship through an innovative, rich curriculum, which responds to children's needs.

*****

Mission Statement from Hillsdale College

Hillsdale College is an independent, non-sectarian institution of higher learning founded in 1844 by men and women "grateful to God for the inestimable blessings" resulting from civil and religious liberty and "believing that the diffusion of learning is essential to the perpetuity of these blessings." It pursues the stated object of the founders: "to furnish all persons who wish, irrespective of nation, color, or sex, a literary and scientific education" outstanding among American colleges "and to combine with this such moral and social instruction as will best develop the minds and improve the hearts of its pupils."

The College considers itself a trustee of modern man's intellectual and spiritual inheritance from the Judeo-Christian faith and Greco-Roman culture, a heritage finding its clearest expression in the American experiment of self-government under law.

By training the young in the liberal arts, Hillsdale College prepares students to become leaders worthy of that legacy. By encouraging the scholarship of its faculty, it contributes to the preservation of that legacy for the future generations. By publicly defending that legacy, it enlists the aid of other friends of free civilization and thus secures the conditions of its own survival and independence.

Aims

Hillsdale College maintains its defense of the

traditional liberal arts curriculum, convinced that it is the best preparation for meeting the challenges of modern life and that it offers to all people of all backgrounds not only an important body of knowledge, but also timeless truths about the human condition. The liberal arts are dedicated to stimulating students' intellectual curiosity, to encourage the critical, well-disciplined mind, and to fostering personal growth through academic challenge. They are a window on the past and a gateway to the future.

The college values the merit of each unique individual, rather than succumbing to the dehumanizing, discriminatory trend of so called "social justice" and "multicultural diversity," which judges individuals not as individuals, but as members of a group and pits one group against other competing groups in divisive power struggles."

If we wish to see how the public school system was used to institute the economic, moral, and governmental changes that the fourth affirmation calls for (which is to integrate the humanist belief system into our "religious, culture, and civilization, as clearly depicted by anthropology and history," and to make this a gradual development that would alter the social heritage, we need look no farther than these statements. The elimination of God leaves the new godless atheism that the secular humanists are striving for. Eventually, the transition, the revolution, would be complete. The reading of John Adams's educational mission statement alongside the current statements reflects this transition.

The education system was targeted as the most aggressive change agent but could not have performed its task without the aid of the court systems. The barrage of cases brought, and still being presented, to challenge our traditional values and spiritual foundations by the ACLU was required. The court system would work to legalize an intolerant state religion of atheism in the state school as well as place a fear of litigation in the hearts and minds of state school administrators. God would no longer be legally allowed in the state school. Private schools may even have limitations and scrutiny if they receive any public funding.

Fear strikes the hearts of school administrations by lawyers who threaten lawsuits. These threats, in turn, convert what may have been freedom-loving administrators from men to mice as they send out questionable edicts for parents and children to conform to humanist demands.

The courts have ruled in favor of secular humanism, imposing the intolerant religion of atheism upon the entire population, and do so by encumbering taxpayers, who likely are unaware their money is being used to instill their children with an atheist worldview.

Books have been written citing individual cases that have now made up a substantial body of law; I will mention two such cases below.

On June 2, 2011, an article by Jim Forsyth printed by Business and Financial News under the line "Valedictorian Fights Judge's Ban on Graduation Prayer" explains the events surrounding a valedictorian of a San Antonio Medina Valley High School asking to lead a prayer at the time she went forward. While the prayer had been a regular part of the graduation ceremony in the past, this year a lawsuit against prayer at the graduation had been filed, so Angela Hildenbrand, who was to have the honor of this year's valedictorian, was told that she would not have the privilege of leading the group in a simple prayer. When asked about her feelings, Hildenbrand said, "After all that I've been taught, about the freedoms of speech, expression, and religion in our country, I am disappointed that my liberties are being infringed upon by this court's ruling to censor my speech." The case had not been decided, but the suit was enforced.

On June 16, 2011, Kyle Gearwar, the valedictorian of Fair Haven Union High School in Vermont, said he was told by school officials that he couldn't include specific information about how God had changed his life in his commencement address. It turned out that the school had the right to censor his address and remove anything that could be construed as proselytizing. Gearwar said the following at the address: "I have always dreamed of speaking about God in front of my school as the valedictorian.

This was the message God gave to me, and I am not allowed to share it with you even though it is my testimony, the most important change my life has ever experienced, and the one thing that I stand for."

These students were stripped of their rights to publicly proclaim God's goodness and provision to their fellow human beings. Our Founding Fathers regularly referred to God and proclaimed His provision. They established daily prayer before every day of public deliberation, which continues today. These examples are *evidence* of the Two Americas we live in. I believe the time has come to unravel these Two Americas, define them, and give them both privilege to thrive. The solutions that will be presented at the end of this book are possible, but they will take a dedication equal to the efforts we have seen by the current humanist revolutionaries.

The Bigger Picture

The fourth affirmation is the guiding philosophy that we find reiterated in the *Humanist Manifesto 2000*. The humanist believes that "all of man's religious culture and civilization" is simply a training of the material man. This leads to the assumption that all cultures and civilizations can be erased and replaced with a one-world government entirely free of God. To achieve their final goal requires retraining the human "animal" within the individual cultures.

Because the goal is a worldwide secular state, international law is encouraged to set legal precedence in the United States. This becomes part of the revolutionary change in America. The world court system will eventually legally require an entirely intolerant life view for all persons in all nations and all cultures. This is one of the reasons that there is a great push by humanists in American politics and jurisprudence to look to international law for our national solutions. This is also why the presidency of Donald Trump's demands for American sovereignty is such an affront and has created such a vehement backlash. Humanists who desire a one-world government support treaties that would compromise our national sovereignty. A nation whose very foundations were built upon biblical principle and belief in God cannot be tolerated. A populace that believes in a prayer-hearing, salvation-providing God is as odious to the secular humanist as the Jews were to Hitler. We will later on see other affirmations that support this statement.

It is interesting to mention once again that the Democratic Party convention of 2012 removed God from the party platform. God was reinstated after causing a public stir; however, the "voice vote" regarding this issue on the floor of the convention, given three separate times, was clear. Three times those in the party ranks who attended the convention were in agreement to remove God from their platform.

In the 2008 film *The Soviet Story*, George Bernard Shaw, the celebrated Progressive playwright, defended Hitler. He advocated killing those who couldn't justify their existence and called for the development of lethal gas—ten years before the National Socialists in Germany did exactly that!

It would logically follow that those who would stand in the way of a philosophy for a perfect, precise state be identified. Those who believe in a prayer-hearing God, a God who saves them, will be considered dangerous. It may be a small step to remove those who refuse to fall into lockstep with an atheist philosophy for the sake of the society. Atheism ultimately will not tolerate any other belief system to exist unless we acknowledge that there are Two Americas and all sides agree that it is time to allow both to live side by side in peace.

The Fifth Affirmation in the *Humanist Manifesto I*

Humanism asserts that the nature of the universe depicted by modern science makes unacceptable any supernatural or cosmic guarantees of human values. Obviously, humanism does not deny the possibility of realities as yet undiscovered, but it does insist that the way to determine the existence and value of any and all realities is by means of intelligent inquiry and by the assessment of their relation to human needs. Religion must formulate its hopes and plans in the light of the scientific spirit and method.

Before discussing the effects of this affirmation on our current society, I wish to reiterate the opening statement of the authors of this document in their introduction, which is as follows:

> The time has come for widespread recognition of the radical changes in religious beliefs throughout the modern world. The time is past for mere revision of the traditional attitudes. Science and economic change have disrupted the old beliefs. Religions the world over are under the necessity of coming to terms with new conditions created by a vastly increasing knowledge and experience. In every field of human activity, the vital movement is now in the direction of the candid and explicit humanism. In order that religious humanism may be better understood we, the undersigned, desire to make certain affirmations which we believe the facts of our contemporary life demonstrates.

Let us remember that the humanism they endeavored to put into place is religious humanism. The atheism proposed by the secular humanists in their world vision is not the atheism of Nietzsche. It is not an atheism without hope and with a certain darkness. They propose a vibrant humanism, which is directed atheism, where all humans actively take part in groups as dedicated as religious organizations, which are established for saving the earth. Remember that the humanist motto is "Doing good without God." This vibrant, new humanism would replace the religious fervor in the human being, essentially giving the citizens a new religious direction. When one observes the dedication of the members of Antifa, one can spot a fervor that has a religious dedication. This is the heart of humanism.

Notice the absolute language utilized in this affirmation: The nature of the universe depicted by modern science makes the old *unacceptable*.

There is no room in the fully evolved society for any belief system other than secular humanism. The humanist way is absolute and intolerant of any other worldview. Have you observed intolerance growing on college campuses, in social media, and in other places? We now have a term we use to describe it—cancel culture. If the worldview does not fit within the humanist system, it is simply eliminated.

This affirmation demands, once again, that there is only one view science may present regarding the nature of the universe. It is an amazingly small perspective of science, and in fact, it contradicts the scientific method. This exclusive view of creation is in stark contrast to many research scientists who are openly making known their wonder regarding the perfection of the design they are discovering.

The movie *Men in Black* comes to mind. The scene where Tommy Lee Jones and Will Smith look into the locker to see an entire universe and then realize that their own universe appears as a "locker" to another universe. Creation is just that remarkable. It is big and intricate and wholly inexplicable. Those who study the individual cell, DNA, the remarkable nature of the eye, the development of a baby in utero, or the amazing reproductive nature of adult stem cells are recognizing the insufficiency of the evolutionary model to explain the complexity of the world around them. Michael Behe, a remarkable biochemist, has studied the cell and published the theory of irreducible complexity. This theory is simply not compatible with evolution. Once one opens the door to his theory, however, it is like opening the locker in the bus station in *Men in Black*— another entire world of study appears. It is scientifically limiting to demand that evolution be our only explanation for existence. Most recently, the noted atheist Richard Dawkins was interviewed for Ben Stein's remarkable documentary *Expelled*. In something that sounds like exasperation, with Ben Stein's probing, Dawkins religiously clings to his absolute belief that there is no God, and finally posits that it is possible that our beginnings sprung from aliens!

TED Talks is a technology site online that has top scientists who give brief talks on various areas of science and technology. While it is a fascinating site, it is difficult to transcribe one of the talks. When talking, the speakers do not necessarily speak in cogent sentences, so when the "talk" is copied exactly, they make for exasperating reading. Nevertheless, I have copied a portion of a talk given by Danny Hillis, who is a noted scientist on the topic "Back to the Future (of 1994)." You can find it online, and I recommend you do so. It is a talk wherein he postulates that we are unable to comprehend how fast information is exponentially growing unless we take a look at how information began, and so he tells a story that satisfies his scientific mind regarding our creation. I have transcribed that talk in part below. To me this talk portrays the absurdity of the evolutionist view of our beginnings.

I am going to have to talk about a bunch of stuff that really doesn't have anything to do with that, because we really have to take a step back and take a long timescale look at things. So the timescale I would like to look at this on is the timescale of life on Earth. So I think this picture makes sense if you look at it a few billion years at a time.

So if you go back about two and a half billion years, the way the chemicals got organized, we begin to get a pretty good idea of how they do it, and I think that there are theories about how RNA started, but I'm going to tell a sort of simple story of it, which is that, at that time, there were little drops of oil floating around with all kinds of different recipes in them. And some of those drops of oil had a particular combination of chemicals in them which caused them to incorporate chemicals from the outside and grow the drops of oil, and those that liked that started to split and divide. And those were the most primitive forms of cells in those little drops of oil. But those little drops of oil were not really alive as we say now, because every one of them was a little random recipe of chemicals, and every time it divided, something different was made. They got sort of unequal division of chemicals within them, and so every drop was a little different. In fact, the drops that were different were what caused them to be better at incorporating chemicals around them. They grew more and incorporated more chemicals and divided more. Those tended to live longer, get expressed more. Now that is sort of a very simple chemical form of life, but when things got interesting was when these drops learned a trick of abstraction, some would say. So what was the next step? Now, by ways that we don't quite understand, the little drops figured out how to write down information—it was the recipe of the cell—onto a particular kind of chemical called DNA. [My observation is to note that these little drops "figured out" a recipe. The anthropomorphism is almost funny.]

So in other words, they worked out in this sort of mindless evolutionary way a form of writing that let them write down what they were so that that way of writing could get copied. The amazing thing is that that way of writing seems to *have stayed steady, since it evolved two and a half billion years ago* [emphasis mine].

In fact, the recipe for us, our genes, is exactly the same code and the same way of writing. In fact, every living creature is written in exactly the same set of letters and the same code.

Then there was a transition. It happened when the communities got close. They decided to write down the whole recipe for the community. In fact, they got together and decided to write string of DNA.

It took about a billion years and the next stage, and at that stage we have multicommunities working together as a single organism. In fact, we're such a multicellular community.

We have lots of cells that are not out for themselves anymore. Your skin cell is really useless without a heart cell, muscle cell a brain cell, and so on. So these communities began to evolve so that the interesting level is that there is no longer a cell but a community, which we call an organism.

Now the next step that happened is, within these communities, these communities of cells again began to abstract information. They began building very special structures that did nothing but write information. It became autocatalytic, something that reinforces its rate of change. The more it changes, the faster it changes, and I think that this is what we are seeing here. [This relates back to changes of information today.]

I, for one, must say that, in my humble opinion, it is far easier and requires much less faith for me to think that there is a designer and to further believe that the design is intricate but consistent and discoverable. The designer's methodology is discoverable and provides information for healing, farming, building, and many other things that can emerge from understanding the design.

It is, however, implausible to my mind that drops of oil billions of years ago "decided" to write their information down and "learned" a trick and so began to express themselves!

The interchange between Stein and Dawkins would have been amusing if it were not so chilling. We find our educational system locked in the clutches of people who are so closed-minded about the universe and so strongly attached to their religious beliefs of atheism that they refuse to see any, and all, evidence to the contrary. In order to cling unquestionably to the supposed "fact" that there is no God, these atheists must postulate the absurd to explain our beginnings and then violate their own scientific methods to adhere to the humanist religious stance! I believe, when one considers the miraculous nature of a single organ, such as the human eye, it requires an ignorance of rational thought not to consider that there was a designer who was at the root of such a complex creation. They must literally ignore every bit of complexity, wonder, and beauty to miss the probability that there is a designer. They need to disregard the miraculous way individual genera and species fit together to form the diversity in our awesome universe.

People of faith don't need to make such a large leap. We have personal histories of God's provision, His deliverance, His presence, and yes, His remarkable creation. His creation writes volumes upon our hearts. Each time we look at the sky, the stars, the moon, the vast colors around us, at the wonder of a worm, a spider, a lizard, our cat, or our child, we are reminded of our Creator. As a citizen or scientist, we see the intricacies of nature and are not afraid or surprised to find a designer at its center.

My personal observation tells me that the atheist lives in a world of black and white, while the theist lives in a world of vivid color. The humanist cannot understand why the theist will not easily be put into their dull box of black and white! I will never attempt to demand that an atheist see my glorious designer, but I am offended that they demand that I block Him out. In the end, whatever "theory" one adopts for our origins is a leap of faith. The humanists/scientists who embrace evolution must make a leap of faith; those who embrace a designer make a leap of faith. As children grow into maturity in our schoolrooms, they should be able to ponder both theories with equal attention and come to their own conclusions.

This exclusive, intolerant, atheistic view of science is successfully curtailing the careers of scientists who are also believers in God from advancing. One recent notable incident occurred on the campus of Emory University. A group of students and professors rallied against the commencement speaker Ben Carson, who is a noted neurosurgeon and humanitarian, author, and Christian. Once the university professors discovered that Dr. Carson had the temerity to oppose their position on evolution and suggest that there was a designer at the heart of the universe, he was denounced in their campus newspaper and shunned. Dr. Carson is a great man, a great healer, and a great thinker of our time, yet the intolerant educators and thought police would destroy him rather than engage him in an intelligent debate—all because he dared to disagree with their singularly religious point of view.

If a student with equal intelligence and gifted abilities as Ben Carson is now coming up through the classes of Emory University, that student would be required to hide their personal belief in order to complete their degree advancement and, ultimately, to practice as a physician and surgeon. Students who will not submit to the intolerant religion of atheism are being blocked from advanced degrees in science.

This fifth affirmation rigorously enacted insists that all the values which we, as a civilized culture, hold true and valuable would bow to the desires of the individual who creates their own value system. Traditional religion must be replaced by a religion of secular humanism, which will ostensibly utilize the scientific method to set public standards.

If the scientific community says there is no God, then it is demanded that the community believe and affirm this "truth." The thoughts and behavior that emanate from a belief in God must be eliminated at any cost. Let us consider just a few of the values that were firmly in place in our culture in 1933 and had their root in Christian thinking.

Honoring parents, honoring one another, truthfulness and honesty (two different things), modesty, industry, thrift, generosity, kindness, control of one's tongue, love, joy, peace, faith, fidelity, contentment, fear of wrongdoing, protection and reverence of life, respect for the union of marriage, respect for the elderly, respect for employers, responsibility to do your best on a job, responsibility to use your personal gifts for God's glory, responsibility to care for one's family, responsibility to save part of your income in order to help those in need, caution against debt to others, responsibility to pay one's debts, management of personal anger by not carrying it to a second day, humility about the future, rejection of worry, respect of property, cleanliness, and modesty.

We were encouraged to "gain" wisdom as well as knowledge. There was encouragement to have discretion and discernment. Husbands were warned against adulteresses and cautioned to drink water from their own cistern. They were also expected to care for their family or be shunned and considered worthless.

These and many other values were commonplace and in common practice in towns and cities all over the country. These values were taught and applied not only at home and in church but in the community at large and certainly in the public school system as well. Of course, every time period and every area of the country has a range of human character, a range of human talent and intelligence. Imperfections abound, but the standards are clear—if not shared, then at least acknowledged. These standards are all an affront to the humanist mind. They are considered out-of-date and harmful to human growth and are contrary to the humanist philosophy of living for the here and now.

The Sixth Affirmation in the *Humanist Manifesto I*

We are convinced that the time has passed for theism deism, modernism, and the several varieties of "new thought."

The signers of this manifesto were purists. They did not desire any mix of religious thought going forward. Their dream was a new country fashioned under the perfect system of atheism. The state religion must be fully implemented. The American Revolution and the writing of the Declaration of Independence made the way available for such a time as this when it said, "Whenever any form of government becomes destructive of these ends, it is the right of the people to alter or to abolish it, and to institute new government." They were ready to put a new governing system into place. This desire for national atheism has been expanded in later humanist documents to a world system dominated by atheism. There would be no room in the nation they were planning for a coexistence of the old and the new. There was to be an entire transformation. It would take time, but they determined to implement their system from the top of the education system down. They would begin with professors at colleges and universities who would prepare the teachers who would teach the children. They would then bring the influence from teachers to their young students, from the students to the parents. The differences between the atheist system postulated by secular humanists and the theistic system expressed in our founding documents and institutions, while seemingly irreconcilable, have lived side by side, each having some space, until now.

In this sixth affirmation, we see that one system must give way to another. Theists have not identified the heart of the revolution, and theists have not attempted to wipe out atheists—nor have they even called them dangerous. Theists appear to be completely unaware of the roots of the battle they are engaged in. Theists believe in freedom and God-given free will. Theists extend to our citizens this free will to choose to accept or deny God, and theists do not demand that atheists embrace a belief in God. The institutionalized, cultural, and legal expressions of our belief in God spring from our very Declaration of Independence, our covenant form of government. They are assumed to be in place and valuable as a social contract, but individual belief in God will never be demanded of a citizen.

The Seventh Affirmation in the *Humanist Manifesto I*

Religion consists of those actions, purposes, and experiences which are humanly significant. Nothing human is alien to the religious. It includes labor, art, science, philosophy, love, friendship, and recreation—all that is in its degree expressive of intelligently satisfying human living. The distinction between the sacred and the secular can no longer be maintained.

This affirmation is singularly interesting and correct. In fact, when one's life is, first and foremost, standing on the unshakable belief in God, all the actions, purposes, and significant experiences are in concert with the will and character of God. They are an expression of faith and trust in God. There is no distinction between how one would think of or treat people on Sunday at church than on Monday, at various businesses or academic endeavors. If we privately profess belief in God, it should smoothly transfer to open faith in God and glory to God in all areas of our lives. Our business, academic, professional, friendship, recreation, hobbies, philosophy, art, and music should reflect our fidelity to God. The humanist will reflect man as their "god" in all areas of life.

The humanists state and recognize that once humanism is successfully employed as the state religion, it will fully engage all areas of social life, the family life, its recreations, friendships, and labors. It will reflect atheism's autonomous rule. I can't help but think of all the children on the soccer and baseball fields on a Sunday morning who have considered their sport in higher regard than a single morning set aside to worship God with friends and family. This practice of instituting Sunday sports activities has quietly turned families away from eligious instruction and relationships within the family of faith. It has established children's sports activities as the point of commonality between families and friends. The transition has been without fanfare, but it has been complete, and the most insidious part of the transition is that those on the field and in the stands on Sunday don't think they have lost any of their Christian commitment.

To one who believes in God, nothing is satisfying apart from having God's presence and principles at work in one's life activities. To the secularist, the sacred must become secular. To the humanist, the secularization must be a national quest.

The Eighth Affirmation in the *Humanist Manifesto I*

Religious humanism considers the complete realization of human personality to be the end of man's life and seeks its development and fulfillment in the here and now. This is the explanation of the humanist's social passion.

To the humanist who believes everything is material and that there is no division of body, mind, and spirit in mankind, there obviously can be no eternity. A later affirmation states that to give people hope of an eternity is "dangerous." This exchange is absolute in principle and breathtaking in scope and practice.

The common Judeo-Christian tenet that would likely be universal in all sects of Christianity and Judaism would be the promise of an eternal life that follows earthly death. This afterlife is likely to be defined differently by different sects, but nearly all share the belief that there will be a personal accounting to a holy God for one's own actions on earth.

Theists commonly apply a cause-and-effect to the concept of an afterlife. They believe this final accounting of their lives will reveal both their love and fealty to the God they serve. This accounting also places a certain reverential fear in the heart of the believer. The book of Proverbs instructs us that "fear of God is the beginning of wisdom."

The Ninth Affirmation in the *Humanist Manifesto I*

In place of the old attitudes involved in worship and prayer the humanist finds his religious emotions expressed in a heightened sense of personal life and in a cooperative effort to promote social well-being.

This affirmation advances the previous affirmation. It describes the *exchange*. In a perfect humanist state, prayer and worship of God will be replaced with a heightened sense of personal life engaged in cooperative effort. Everyone will *feel* like their lives are heightened by belonging to a cooperative effort to "promote social well-being." The current educational indoctrination of schoolchildren is the result of this affirmation. Children are taught of the need for them to be involved in saving the environment at the earliest possible age. This affirmation was exemplified in the 2008 presidential election, with elementary school children who were taught to sing adoring songs about then presidential hopeful Barack Obama. The children made banners and had any manner of activities around the presidential hopeful, including topics such as environmental awareness. Their emotions were heightened in relation to the political personality of the presidential hopeful. They were excited about a hope and social change that they had no real understanding of. The children were not given a balance of information about the nation, nor were they given the tools of analytical thinking that would allow them to understand the complexity of problems, or the breadth of solutions. This revolutionary army is built on feeling good about what they are doing. The leader's goal is to encourage children to have an emotional investment in the cause with which they are presented. The teachers are willing to use the children as a means to their political and social ends. This trained emotional response will teach children to be moldable into community groups, which allows the elite a control of resources.

The children unwittingly become a part of the revolution (please see the appendix for the Children's Bill of Rights). The politics of personality are similar to the personality that led the German revolution of 1939. Children are taught to be activists and citizens of the world. These aspirations are supported in music, art, and special project days. This social indoctrination done, in the name of education, will be the childhood memories that tie the culture together.

Special Events Make for Everyday Indoctrination Opportunities or Christmas in the Boonies

Once again, I would like to digress to a little personal story.

I was invited to my granddaughter's school last Christmas for a play. The play was done near the Christmas break, and in times past, it would have been a Christmas play with a combination of sacred and fun Christmas songs. A few years back, it could have had some small vestige of the celebration of Christmas. This play, for me, was a picture of how far the revolution has traveled, how deeply ingrained it is, and how difficult it is to battle.

The play was put on by a "traveling group" who received funding to go into schools and work with the children for *one week*. The group brought in the costumes, the sets, the music, the script, and the *social indoctrination*. The actors and directors were funded outside of the elementary school; I did not look into their funding source. The name of the play was *The Hare and the Tortoise*, adapted from the Aesop fable of the same name. The play was pure humanist indoctrination. The original Aesop fable was designed to instill the character quality of perseverance. The original fable teaches the hearts of the reader that the prize does not always go to the swift and gifted but can go to the one who is steady and perseveres. The original fable reaches the heart of the child in the classroom that may not be the most beautiful or seemingly the most talented. It gives them hope to persevere. Those who read the original *The Hare and the Tortoise* believe that if they work hard and are steady and persistent, they can win the race. Conversely, it teaches the child with natural ability and talent that "pride comes before a fall." These simple and time-honored truths were *exchanged* in the play I attended.

The "new" *The Hare and the Tortoise*, which replaced a traditional Christmas program, is significant because it will become part of the children's shared life experience. It will become their memory of commonly held values and a tie for the community. Here is a synopsis.

A media personality is now the central figure in the play (what a surprise!). The newscaster comes into town to cover the annual race between the lizards and the mammals. The lizards and mammals have a historic contention that divided the town. The division is between the mammals, including such things as the furry, cute bunny families, as well as others, and the reptiles, which included lizards and, of course, the tortoise. The play opens with the newscaster front and center, ready to announce the event. She discusses the two sides in the race, their historic contention, and then discusses the characteristics of the two individual groups.

The mammals are portrayed as the more powerful group, but the ones with evil intentions and prideful actions (think Capitalists). The lizards and reptiles, though not as beautiful, are portrayed as the good and steady folk. They support the rainbow coalition between scenes as the children sing songs of unity.

The mean mammals are intent on winning, and the rabbit, who would compete in the race, is arrogant and unkind. The mammals also promote the continued segregation of animals. Chief among the evil mammals owns a gas station—can you imagine that! (Isolating people into groups of victims is a specialty of humanists.)

The race finally begins with the media personality setting the social tone. The tragedy of the day occurs when one of the little bunnies gets lost. The loss pulls the entire community together as one (unity); the race is completely changed, and both the tortoise and the hare come across the finish line together. No one wins—so the message is, *everyone* wins. The older mammals and reptiles that have set up the "racist" society are led by the children to love and embrace one another. So much for instilling true and proper competition and perseverance, where the race goes to the humble who work hard.

This play divided people into small groups defined by differences and created victim status by virtue of the birthright. (This pictured both racism and homophobia.) It contrasted the victims to the bullying society. The bullies were portrayed as ones who devalued the victims. It further redefined the family as anyone we get together with. The family of man can be lizards and bunnies or any other combination. The choice of the media person as the focal point promoted the media to the status of social healer. The newscaster exchanged the position of journalist for the job of a social change agent who, like the traveling preacher of days gone by, rallied all the people together in the end. The media personality was the leader, the good guy, the one with insight and persistence to bring everyone together. She was the peacemaker who led the song of unity with the previously intolerant society. The final indoctrination was that the children must lead, not follow. The children must become actively involved in the revolution to set parents on the right road. Aesop's original *The Tortoise and the Hare* theme simply teaches children that anyone can win if they are persistent. This play was truly a work of indoctrination. The play ended with all the kids on the stage, the newscaster front and center, under a rainbow, portraying the new family, where a lizard and a bunny were now a new family.

Being the grandma that I am, I could not help analyzing every word, every song, and every principle of indoctrination. It nearly brought me to tears. This school had corrupted my grandchildren's minds and hearts. They had robbed them of Christmas memories that should have been filled with rousing renditions of "Silent Night" and "Jolly Old Saint Nicholas" and presented this play wholly designed for social engineering. I was completely unprepared for this because the public school my grandchildren attend has a large number of Christian teachers; it is a small community, and I had previously thought it was a conservative community of ranchers.

When the play was over, I put on my happy face, hugged my

grandchildren, and told them what a wonderful job they had done. It would serve no purpose to make them feel that the hard work they put in throughout the week was attached to something that opposed their family core values.

I am not certain that there was another person in the audience that "got" what was transpiring. I understood it because I am aware of the secular humanist tenets and the revolution that is taking place. Those who read this book will be able to fill a new book with stories similar to mine that they have witnessed in their own schools. This seemingly innocuous indoctrination is an ongoing process in the public school system, and we will either endorse by default or begin to take a new look at public education.

This was a perfect example of the exchange of old attitudes involved in worship (the acknowledgment of the miraculous Christmas story) to a heightened sense of personal life and cooperative effort to promote well-being.

The *Humanist Manifesto II* updates this affirmation. As we approach the specifics of the *Humanist Manifesto II*, that personal life bows to the cooperative on an entirely new level. In the second manifesto, we find that our free market economy based on Capitalism must be replaced with Socialism. The *Humanist Manifesto 2000* completes the exchange of individualism for the good of the cooperative. These exchanged roots are in this ninth affirmation of *Humanist Manifesto I* and will ultimately grant the power to government to redistribute all the world's resources according to the good of the cooperative. As world government embraces the power to redistribute resources and allocate to individuals their just due, national sovereignty will be obliterated, the cooperative will be enforced, and the state will be the supreme authority over all. They are very close to moving the humanist worldview in to control our nation and utterly silence the church. Victory is within their grasp.

And then the unthinkable occurs. Trump is elected president. He vows to preserve national sovereignty and religious freedom, reinvigorate our Capitalistic economic system, allow for school choice, and even to grant Israel their capital in Jerusalem. This is a declaration of all-out war!

The frustration for the humanists was that they anticipated the change was to be completed in a Hillary presidency. The state was to be supreme. The church influence in family lives was to be silenced. Providing for the poor, counseling people in stress, and helping families were to become the work of the secular state. The U.S. was to decrease in financial strength and world power to prepare for its fall to the one world government agency.

The Tenth Affirmation in the *Humanist Manifesto I*

It follows that there will be no uniquely religious emotions and attitudes of the kind hitherto associated with belief in the supernatural.

Will you join me in considering that this is perhaps the second most dangerous affirmation to individual freedoms? It is *terrifying* to note that this dangerous, unconstitutional principle is being set into law every day. Eliminating the uniquely religious emotions for the supernatural describes a work in the heart and spirit of a person. This is the underlying principle for the work of both the thought police and the speech police. This is beyond thought control—it suggests control of emotions and attitudes. This can be done because pure humanist thought does not acknowledge anything but the material. They do not see or believe that the spirit of an individual may be touched by the Spirit of the living God. Anyone who walks by faith and has a history of God's work in their lives would disagree in this purely material worldview.

Consider for one moment the power of an intolerant state religion that would demand that your uniquely religious emotions and attitudes align strictly with their dictates and the faith of atheism. An example of this would be a kindergarten boy coming home from a California schoolroom where they have been introduced to the concept that they may, in fact, be a girl. The family values would inform the child that they are created in God's image for His purpose and have been created a boy. This theistic religious conviction is at odds with the state's religion of atheism and the state's religious tenets of humanism. If the parents will not endorse, they may find that their son is taken from them and put in a home that will comply. If they fight too strenuously, they may find themselves in jail. All theistic personal convictions and emotions are to be eliminated from your life, from your national life, and from public discourse.

How, you might ask, can this happen in America? The answer is simple. The plan to bring about an intolerant atheist revolution in America, which includes a change in our history, sociology, family structure, educational institutions, economic structure, and national sovereignty, has been written, implemented, and accepted by the ruling class. It is yet to be seen how many Christians agree. The plan was set afoot many years ago, and as the winds of the revolution blow louder and harder every day, the demands that the vestiges of theism must be removed are legion. They issue forth from the media in concert with the ACLU.[3] The demands that our emotions be aligned with secular humanist doctrines are felt in the workplaces and schools every day.

I want to go to the news of the day and mention three laws that were put into place in California several years ago.

SB-1172. A piece of legislation that bans gay-to-straight therapy for minors has now become law in California. The instruction and well-being of minor children has previously been considered the responsibility of parents. In the event that a minor child has been introduced to homosexual behavior, a parent, up until now, has been given the responsibility to care for the child in light of their own family belief system. This could include counseling by pastors and Christian counselors about the biblical framework of differentiation between male and female and the admonition against homosexuality. This law usurps the position of parents and parental authority in the lives of minor children. It dictates the beliefs, emotions,

---

[3] American Civil Liberties Union. The nonprofit group that uses the courts and turns our own law, which provides civil liberties, against us and establishes atheism and eliminates theism.

and training of the child and must be aligned with humanist doctrines and not be allowed to be weighed against traditional Judeo-Christian beliefs. This presumes that the humanist perspective of homosexuality is healthy and that it would be wrong for parents or any other person to question it. In light of this law, parents would no longer be allowed to train their children in the uniquely religious beliefs and emotions of their traditional faith. These would be uniformly replaced with the intolerant religion of secular humanism. This is another illustration of the need to entirely silence the Christian voice. The humanist is not content to allow the systems to be judged side by side by the individual. Theism must be silenced.

The child raised in a family of faith where there are unique beliefs in a supernatural God has been informed that their beliefs and emotions will be prohibited from bringing those beliefs and instructions to bear in their child's life at this crucial juncture. In this instance, the state religion of secular humanism, which believes in a material here and now and no eternal consequences, demands that the minor child be left to pursue what a parent could believe is a tragic direction. At this writing, the governor of New Jersey has also signed a similar bill into law.

S-B1476. A measure that will allow children in the state to have more than two parents. Even if one does not consider the role of an absent parent as the parent of a child, a theistic position must acknowledge two biological parents. A man and a woman who provide the DNA and the hereditary genetic structure that bring forth a child. A theist believes that each child has a purpose and is created and loved by God. A theist acknowledges that the parents of the child make a difference even if they are absent from the child's life. One of our children is adopted. We consider ourselves to be her parents but recognize that her DNA, her genetic code, has some similarities to her biological parents. While we trained behaviors and beliefs into our daughter, her entire individual makeup was God's design through the joining of her biological parents. To deny that parenthood is another arena of denying God. Everything to the humanist may be defined by his own logic rather than absolute truth, including biology. This law demonstrates the indoctrination in the play that I just mentioned, children redefining the family unit by whatever standards they choose.

SB-623 is the third bill, which may be law in California by the time this book is available. This measure will allow nurses to perform abortions. This may not appear to be a direct assault on the religious emotions and does not, in and of itself, attack one for having uniquely religious attitudes toward the Creator, but in the end it will have a great deal to do with the practical living of a theist. A man or woman in the nursing program of a state university who believes that performing abortion is the taking of a life may, in the future, be kept from a nursing career if their "uniquely religious emotions and attitudes" are contrary to this intolerant secular humanist state religion. In the event a nursing student will not agree to both study and participate in abortion, they may be eliminated from the profession. It is wise to consider, once again, that a gifted surgeon like Ben Carson would likely not be allowed into the profession.

The cases arising out of this one affirmation are ubiquitous and well-documented in other books and magazines. Our purpose is to identify why these cases exist—their genesis, if you will. Our purpose is also to observe the current effects and project the effects of each affirmation as the revolution is completed. In this case, there will be a complete lack of tolerance toward any expression or emotion that includes God as He is portrayed in the Bible and believed by millions of Americans, both Jewish, Christian, and theists. Currently, college students who hold uniquely religious emotions and attitudes in regards to abortion, have been disallowed advancement in some medical programs. Children in public education are ridiculed for their belief in creation science, and some are held back or failed. I know a secretary at a local automobile dealership who had spiritual content on the screensaver who was called a bigot and homophobe and, in the end, lost her chance of advancement. She was neither a bigot nor a homophobe and pretty much kept her views to herself, except to be kind and overly tolerant to the demands around her in the workplace. Her faults were an undeniable love of God and Jesus as her Savior, coupled with a naivete regarding the world around her. She was unaware of the exchange taking place around her, which demanded her uniquely religious emotions and attitudes be hidden from view while in public, which will eventually ensure a loyalty to secular humanism. She was unaware that she no longer had a right to express her love of Jesus in her workplace or her private computer.

This type of harassment has been an effective way of subduing personal expressions of faith as well as suppressing spiritual emotions. This is not an isolated workforce incident but is also repeated in hundreds of ways each and every day in the state school system.

The fear of social reprisal has had the effect of silencing the theist, and especially the Christian, while there is public demand that every other group be affirmed, outed, and approved.

Who Are the Real Workplace Bullies?

You Must Comply!

I recently had a conversation with a man in his late thirties. He is a highly admired professional in his company. He holds a PhD in the sciences. The company he works for is huge and receives government contracts. Since the government has its hand in the business, they have the government-imposed social restructuring (the revolution of the state religion of atheism being instituted).

In an entirely private setting, he recently made mention to me that he is "tired of the homosexual agenda being forced down his throat." His statement, spoken in exasperation, went something like, "I don't run around telling everyone I am a heterosexual in a committed marriage, I don't force them to approve or appreciate my choice, and I just do my work." This statement spoke volumes to me. It spoke volumes about the "tolerance" demanded of each and every person in order for this "intolerant" dogma to suffocate our nation. What provides affirmation for one may be a muzzle to another. We need to move beyond this.

The aggressive political agenda of the homosexual joined with the transexual movement will be the arm of the secular humanist movement which will secure the demand for "no uniquely religious emotions and attitudes of the kind hitherto associated with the belief in the supernatural."

Most theists who acknowledge and believe in a Creator will acknowledge that His design is male and female and that the design is specific for the purpose of procreation. The design is to create strong family units. The family unit, in the mind of the theist, is responsible to raise, feed, clothe, train, instruct, love, and laugh with their children. The benefit, hopefully, will be to enjoy their children. To watch them grow, be happy, be financially secure, and be involved in their families into the future. The theist hopes to raise balanced, faithful children they can be proud of. Many theists are familiar with verse 3 found in Psalm 127, "Lo, children are a heritage of the Lord: and the fruit of the womb is his reward."

It is in this very arena that the government has now instituted a new definition of marriage, a new definition of parent, and a new definition of family. Citizens will now have the force of law demand that they accept and approve of this moral arrangement. No uniquely held religious emotions or attitudes will any longer be acceptable. Family life, now legally governed by this tenth affirmation, will demand that, in addition to acceptance of the new morality, it become illegal to have deeply held religious beliefs and emotions that would cause one to raise children with the instruction of God's pattern for the "family." Thus, the uniquely religious emotions and attitudes will have completed the exchange from the traditional theist-held belief system to the secular humanist belief system.

If you, dear reader, think for a second that this cannot happen, take a long look at the change in law and social structure of the past three years. You will see that that force of law grows stronger each day to compel you to comply.

The Eleventh Affirmation in the *Humanist Manifesto I*

Man will learn to face the crises of life in terms of his knowledge of their naturalness and probability. Reasonable and manly attitudes will be fostered by education and supported by custom. We assume that humanism will take the path of social and mental hygiene and discourage sentimental and unreal hopes and wishful thinking.

The means to the end described in this affirmation is found in public education, entertainment, public discourse, and law. Reasonable and manly attitudes will be found by people set free from hope in God, hope in prayer, and expectation of heaven. Reason would instruct the mind of man to be fulfilled, to live life to its utmost. Sickness and death are part of the process and are to be accepted without being irrationally attached to a hope in the supernatural.

A recent interview with a noted neurosurgeon will give some bright light on this affirmation. The neurosurgeon said that his profession, in terms of medical dollars, is the most expensive medical specialty. He noted that much of their work is done on an emergency basis (think stroke!). The doctors are required to work quickly and decisively.

He attended a professional seminar where they were covering some of the details and changes that could be expected when Obamacare was fully enforced. He noted that throughout the seminar, the word *person* or *patient* was no longer used; instead, the government had *exchanged* the terms *person* or *patient* with the term *government unit*. By dehumanizing the patient to the doctor, they were accomplishing the task of treating the government unit apart from the sentimentality demanded by the theist mindset. They were instructed that the "government unit" who exceeds seventy be kept comfortable, but the expense of a neurosurgeon's care would not be extended without an extensive panel review of their case.

Let's get this picture under twenty-twenty vision. It is eleven o'clock at night. Your husband, who is otherwise healthy, begins to act in an odd way. He can't smile, his arm hurts, he can't tell you his name, and he can't get on his feet. You either call an ambulance or rush him to a hospital yourself. All your education instructs you that this could be a stroke, and early intervention in a stroke situation is everything. You take him in the hospital door. The hospital staff recognizes an emergency, gets him in a room, and you begin to give them his insurance card and his information. They note that his birth date is 1941. The quick action stops; you are ushered from the room with the understanding that they will care for him. He is given something intravenously to make him "comfortable" while the stroke takes its full toll. Could this be our future? Could the worthiness of a "unit" to live expire at age seventy?

Preparation for These Decisions Right Under Our Noses

The humanist state education system prepares us to make these "manly" decisions. A lovely young seventh grader I know, who is extremely bright and a dedicated Christian, told me of a writing assignment she was given in an English class last year. The teacher had assigned an essay wherein she posed a scenario where five people were in a boat that was adrift at sea with no hope in sight. They had enough supplies for four people to live for eight days, but if they fed five people, they would survive only six and a half days. The assignment was to write an essay explaining which people should be kept and which should be discarded, based on their value to the community of people left. The people consisted of a doctor, a young mother, an old retired person, a retarded person, and a singer. I have heard of variations on this little social strategy for thirty years, so I was not surprised that she had been given the assignment of determining who should live and who should die. This particular girl has Asperger's syndrome, and she has a grandparent in his nineties who is still very bright and capable and to whom she is very close. The surprise for me was how quickly she determined who was expendable and that this school exercise did not seem offensive or unusual either to herself, her Christian parents, or her Christian grandparents. We are, for the most part, blind to the revolution going on under our own roof. Let us return back to our neurosurgeon. Currently, neurosurgeons are available on staff at hospitals for just such emergencies. The future may be quite different. *If* the future allows for on-staff neurosurgeons, they may be unable to proceed in an emergency manner without a panel agreement. The usefulness of the government unit may become the basis upon which treatment is given or withheld.

The reasonable and "manly" thing to do is to consider the quality of life from the atheist perspective to determine if *collective* funds should be spent on a seventy-year-old to extend his life.

These "manly" and reasonable views have been part of the social engineering in our atheistic public school system for many years. It is assumed that the professionals, having been indoctrinated in state schools, will be able to express these manly views and decisions with relative ease.

The foundational training to make decisions such as this may be occurring in your fourth grader's class even today. Consider the boat assignment that I described. This exercise trains the young mind to think of life and death and the actual killing of someone in their immediate company for the sake of the collective. This instills an atheist thinking process in determining life-and-death questions and gives these decisions into the hands of very young people.

The *situational ethics* taught at all grade levels in the state school system eliminates the presence of an absolute authority. Removing God gives any individual the authority to make life-and-death decisions. In fact, all decisions will be based on the good of the collective. This trains both mind and heart to place a value on the people around them based wholly on their potential contribution to the overall collective. At a time of scarce resources, the fully indoctrinated secular humanist will be prepared for the manly, reasonable response called for by the secular humanist revolutionaries.

The person raised with a conscience toward God would make a decision to give up their own lives to save another. Self-sacrifice and self-denial would mirror the life of Jesus. Faith that God sees, hope that He will deliver, and love of one another and God would draw the people in the boat together, not isolate them from one another.

We then conclude that theists who do not conform will be sorted out of the medical professions at the college level to bring about the secular age. The new medical practitioners must be willing to make a *unit* comfortable so that they will not be a burden on the *collective*.

The theist would, following Dylan Thomas's beautiful poem, rage against death on behalf of their patients, doing battle until the end. They could not let people go "quietly into that good night" apart from exercising their reasonable, trained skill to save the person's lives. A theist who is a doctor would battle every foe for their patient. They do not count the patient's worth or their value to the collective; rather, they are trained to save lives wherever they can.

On a practical level, this battle for the lives of patients is blown into a raging conflict in the medical world. This conflict is currently taking place between the state dictates and the doctors who, aware of how to save lives in the battle with the coronavirus, are threatened with the loss of their license should they use a benign medication that has a forty-year track record for safety. They have found it to be a completely safe and effective means of keeping their patients alive. The powers in control of this disease do not want treatment to come into play. We may wonder why such a battle rages, but if we have clarity regarding the end goal of the *Humanist Manifesto*, it is obvious that the reason is that the one-world elites want a vaccine for population control.

These great doctors and nurses wage war against disease, accident, and old age until the moment when the last breath, in its great final sigh, leaves the patient's body and the soul begins its final journey. In the age to come, the patients' war against death will be defined for them in humanist terms. Obamacare ushered that mindset into the medical field.

The Twelfth Affirmation in the *Humanist Manifesto I*

Believing that religion must work increasingly for joy in living, religious humanists aim to foster the creative in man and to encourage achievements that add to the satisfaction of life.

This sounds like a wonderful affirmation and one all of us could embrace. The humanist religion put into place as the state religion would foster the creative arts. Theater, music, and the arts should be provided ample government encouragement and funding to ensure an opportunity for citizens to pursue their artistic desire. The National Endowment for the Arts, funding national TV and radio, funding national radio commercials, tax-funded artists, studies, and grants would be proliferated under the national religion of secular humanism—as they have been these past twenty-plus years.

The roads near where I live have been in the process of being widened and upgraded over the past five years. I went to a few of the public meetings and discovered at one of them that 1 percent of the money allocated to the project to widen and restore our roads had been allocated for "art" to be commissioned and installed along the roadside. It does not sound like much, but the size of the road budget was enormous, so 1 percent was also an enormous amount. The citizens could have their input as to what they were interested in seeing. We overwhelmingly chose horses as a theme and hence have a rather-lovely sculpture of a horse and foal in the median between the roads.

What does this have to do with the *Humanist Manifesto*? The manifesto aims to foster creativity in man. This is not a bad idea, but again, the man is to replace religion and faith in a prayer-hearing God with "creativity." It is to fill the religious void in his life. Government has become very interested in funneling public monies to artists over the past seventy years. The roads near my home are an example. The art on our road is lovely and recognizable. Where there was no public input, the art is formless, aimless, and rainbow-colored, but the public funds were allocated to the local artists of the bureaucracy's choice.

It would be interesting to trace the government funding of art over the past sixty years and to ascertain what attitudes and belief systems the public monies have favored. We do know that when Adolf Hitler brought the Third Reich into power, they recognized the power of art. They acknowledged that most artists were individualist. They had a goal of completely wiping out individualism. To reach this goal, in *s*, page 208, author Richard J. Evans states this:

> The Soviet Union and Nazi Germany waged an unremitting war on individualism, proclaiming art's only acceptable function to be the expression of the soul of the masses. Art was to be used to mobilize the spirit and to help to conquer the will of the people.

In addition to this direct support to fund the arts, I believe that the national mind is becoming more emotionally motivated (artistic) in its decision-making in the areas of education, politics, and certainly, economics. The ability to think critically and logically is being lost in the revolutionary process. The public education process is frequently attentive to what a child thinks and feels rather than what is. Hence, at a time of economic crisis, we currently spend most of our political time debating emotional issues rather than attempting to bring about a rational process to recover our economic prosperity and national strength. (Oh yes, we must remember that under the humanist revolution, we no longer wish to be a strong, independent nation.)

In truth, the logical mind would eliminate emotionally driven arguments that currently allocate vast amounts of national funds.

The Thirteenth Affirmation in the *Humanist Manifesto I*

Religious Humanism maintains that all associations and institutions exist for the fulfillment of human life. The intelligent evaluation, transformation, control [italics mine] and direction of such associations and institutions with a view to the enhancement of their ritualistic forms, ecclesiastical methods and common activities must be co constituted as rapidly as experience allows, in order to function effectively in the modern world.

This suggests that churches, clubs, and organizations with traditional beliefs and secular organizations who have traditionally Judeo-Christian roots, including prayer or invocations, would be evaluated, transformed, and controlled. A secular humanist society going forward demands the replacement be complete. This allows that there be churches but the churches would support and perform same-sex marriages, would conform the scriptures to the new humanist narrative, which would ultimately deny the existence of the God of the Bible, and in all ways, would support the secular humanist doctrines.

In order to facilitate the exchange, secular humanists must take all groups, both social and religious, and "co-constitute" or bring them into humanist thought. This means secular humanists are to join churches, clubs, and organizations that have traditional values at the top levels and begin to inform the future direction, behavior, and beliefs of those organizations. In this way, the advancement of humanist policy will be instituted at the YMCA, at the World Council of Churches, at high levels of university and school system, at the Boy Scouts and the Knights of Columbus. The atheist "religious" zeal and social passion thrust individual zealots from the college classroom into the social structure to move into key positions in organizations and churches throughout the country. As you read this, you will note that the Boy Scouts of America, who fought back the onslaught for years, has given way to the intolerant secular humanists who refuse a private organization to hold and affirm Judeo-Christian views. The Boy Scouts, in just a few short years, is now in full-blown surrender and, as such, has regained the corporate funding that was pulled during their attempt to retain a conservative, God-centered organization. The Boy Scouts have paid a high price in legal costs every year for that freedom to remain outside of the secular humanist state edicts. Every vestige of Christian belief in relation to homosexual activity has been driven from the organization, and the organization and its members are in full compliance with this eleventh secular humanist affirmation.

The ongoing legal harassment of this traditional organization does not make much sense to the average citizen unless they are familiar with this document and comprehend that the pillars in society must fall in order for the revolution to be complete. The humanists target areas where lawsuits can be successful. They may select a child as their puppet to provide the material for a suit. The Boy Scouts finally succumbed to the political, financial, and legal pressure in the summer of 2013. As of February 2017, the Boy Scouts welcomed transgender "boys" and are now wearing rainbow knots to indicate solidarity.

The secular humanists know how to strategically choose their battles, and they knew this was a battle they must win at any cost.

Another arena the secular humanists have actively engaged is the Christian Church. The doctrines of social justice are now regularly a part of spiritual instruction. Classes like the sojourners (for seniors) and Sunday school material drenched in equality and social justice rather than Bible teaching have been instituted in the many conservative, ecclesiastic churches without question.

The materials used at your Sunday schools may mirror the current social trends but may be sadly lacking in biblical instruction and encouragement of the exercise of faith, hope, and love.

Children's Sunday school material may be questionable. The materials may copy the same social beliefs taught in public schools, such as environmentalism, and approved social restructuring, such as a curriculum about bullying that introduces homosexuality and transgender children as potentially the target of bullying. This not only introduces this lifestyle but also garners a certain sympathy toward it. The same Sunday school may be sadly lacking in the instruction of the Ten Commandments, the substitutionary death of Christ for the world's sin, and other basic tenets. Theists ought, in fact, to be environmentalists, because they are stewards of God's earth. Theists, above all people, should be in awe and wonder at God's great creation; they should treat the creation with respect, but they should reject any attempt to presume they are the ultimate arbitrator of the end of the planet. They should always reject an exchange of worship of the creation in place of worship of the Creator.

The Fourteenth Affirmation in the *Humanist Manifesto I*

The humanists are firmly convinced that existing acquisitive and profit—motivated society has shown itself to be inadequate and that a radical change in methods, controls and motives [italics mine] must be instituted. A socialized and cooperative economic order must be established to the end that the equitable distribution of the means of life be possible [italics mine]. The goal of humanism is a free and universal society in which people voluntarily and intelligently cooperate for the common good. Humanists demand a shared life in a shared world." [This has been copied directly from their text without the benefit of editing.]

Notice, again, the absolute intolerant language used: "Radical change in methods, controls and motives must be instituted"; a socialized and cooperative economic order must be established. Humanists *demand* a shared life.

Oh, that our free economy thinkers could be so unshakable and absolute!

This affirmation and the effects of the affirmation are self-evident. The areas of law, education, and entertainment have been utilized to drive public opinion to accept and affirm the redistribution of wealth worldwide to achieve a "means of life" for all people and for the "common good." The curriculum of social justice at all levels of state education, university, and public and private workplaces abounds. This affirmation seeks to do the following:

1. Undermine and remove our economic system and make the exchange of the *free market* system for a *Socialist state.*

2. Appoint the government as the arbiter of all private wealth and allow the state to redistribute personal wealth for the common good. The United States must fall before the redistribution could be instituted worldwide. The state schools are training the upcoming generations to hate the attitudes of individualism and to embrace collective thought and behavior, to embrace social justice, and to believe that redistribution of wealth from our nation to other nations is a right and just thing to do.

3. This affirmation is clarified in both the *Humanist Manifesto II* and the *Humanist Manifesto 2000.* There is no doubt that the revolutionaries, once their work is complete in the US, will expect to hand America over to a one-world government.

4. The "means of life" are mentioned here but will later be enumerated.

5. A crucial point in this affirmation is that humanists *demand* "a shared life and a shared world." Though they state, "The desire for a free and universal society where people voluntarily and intelligently cooperate," it is clear that they *demand* people to live in a shared life and a shared world. This pictures redistribution at any cost. This agenda demands the full indoctrination of all students to the Socialist global agenda. It demands that American children be ashamed of American prosperity and have their hopes and dreams for their own prosperity silenced. It demands that this intolerant worldview be taught at all levels, from preschool to university. It also demands that those

who disapprove or are uncooperative be removed so that the advancement of the humanist agenda will not be hampered.

6. The worldwide economic system fostered by secular humanists will reflect the lords and servants, or slaves and masters, spoken of earlier.

The 2020 presidential race illustrated the shift in our collective economic thought more than anything else I can point to. One candidate, Donald Trump, has worked at the top levels of the free enterprise system with great success. He was experienced in handling corporate projects. He was experienced in the development of budgets and in job creation. The United States is in a crisis in all these areas. This candidate illustrated success as a parent. He is a man who is intelligent and well spoken. The single characteristic that appeared to be his biggest negative was that he had been a successful American businessman! His successes led him to substantial personal wealth, which was intolerable! His wealth, which would once have been an indicator of a keen business mind, was distrusted and looked upon with derision.

His business acumen and thorough working knowledge of the free enterprise system was exactly what the world citizens trained by the humanist blueprint of this good nation did not want. They wanted a person in power who had lived their entire life in the government system, who had gotten wealthy not through the free enterprise system but rather through manipulating their government position.

The previous eight years the voters had chosen a man fully indoctrinated in secular humanism, they chose a leader steeped in redistribution, social justice, and social programs. The shift to Donald Trump in 2016 as a businessman and a leader who loves our national sovereignty and freedom of religion and recognizes the shift away from Judeo-Christian principles has been a refreshing surprise. The 2020 election will speak volumes about what our citizens think and what they believe.

The traditional thinker recognizes the difference between the current president, who has gained his wealth through the competitive, rough-and-tumble business as a builder, and the past president, who now is vastly wealthy but whose résumé contains being a community organizer, one-term senator, and president for eight years, with his highest salary being the presidential salary of $400,000 per year. This man now owns three palatial mansions and is worth multimillions of dollars. In comparing the two men and their rise to wealth, one can only speculate how the later accrued his assets.

The Fifteenth and Last Affirmation in the *Humanist Manifesto I*

We assert that humanism will (a) affirm life rather than deny it, (b) seek to elicit the possibilities of life not flee from it and (c) endeavor to establish the conditions of a satisfactory life for all [italics mine], not merely for a few. By this positive morale and intention humanism will be guided, and from this perspective enlightenment and techniques and efforts of humanism will flow.

So stand the theses of religious humanism. Though we consider the religious forms and ideas of our fathers no longer adequate, the quest for the good life is still the central task for mankind. Man is at last becoming aware that he alone is responsible for the realization of the world of his dreams, that he has within himself the power for its achievement. He must set intelligence and will to the task.

This final affirmation restates the government's right to redistribute personal wealth. This affirmation, which calls for personal responsibility, in essence, calls for citizens to fall into lockstep at the government's command—i.e., to redistribute the national personal and international wealth for the good of the collective. Personal freedoms will be a vague memory when this affirmation is fully implemented. It is right at the door. The transformation is nearly here.

When the State Religion of Atheism is Fully Instituted, the Declaration of Independence will have been Officially Annulled

Having completed this initial document of the revolution, you, the reader, may not need to go any further to understand it. You may see clearly the place from which we have come and the road that we have taken. If you have never read or heard of this document, you may be surprised. If you are aware of this manifesto, you may now be more informed about how we arrived at our current place in history. You may now understand the motivation for the specific legislative, legal, and educational objectives that are being instituted each and every day. You may see the battle lines and the controversies more clearly. Some call these people Progressives, some call them Liberals, but unfortunately, none of those titles will reveal the doctrines the revolutionaries are living and the specific, line-upon-line dictates they must bring about to complete the revolution. You may have been unaware that there is a specific road we are traveling. You may have been unaware of the *intolerant* "religion" of atheism that is being adopted as a state religion. You may be unaware that at the time atheism is accepted nationally, the Declaration of Independence, which asserts a covenant form of government, will be officially *over*. More importantly, you may be unaware that we could yet pull back and stop this forward movement.

What can we do to change directions? When we complete the second manifesto, we will consider some very practical suggestions that can be implemented to stop the forward motion and to inhibit the humanists from their national religion exchange.

To summarize:

1. The religious humanists desire

    a. to completely remove God from our institutions and private lives,

    b. to redefine theist belief systems with atheist belief,

c. to institute atheism as an unquestioned state religion,

d. to fully exchange our traditional belief in God with the tenets stated in both *Humanist Manifesto*, and

e. to permeate every level and every interest in society with secular humanism.

The tenets require that secular humanism be religiously adhered to; there will be complete intolerance toward any other religious system that includes a prayer-hearing God or the need for salvation.

2. To use our current tolerant legal system to establish the religious secular humanist legal system, thus making atheism the state religion. (There would be an exchange of theism in any of its various forms or sects in our educational systems with atheism. This new atheism promises freedom but delivers tyranny such as Americans have never seen.

3. To remove all religious traditions from society. All religious holidays or symbols that carry Judeo-Christian religious significance would be removed. Muslim images and religious practice will be encouraged, as it also is an enemy of Judaism and Christianity. These holidays and symbols will be exchanged for national holidays and events that are supportive of secular humanism. People will be encouraged to have a "religious zeal" for communal purposes. The new spiritual service will be environmental days, sexual activists' days, and World Day or Global Environment Day. Each of these celebrations will be supportive of the secular humanist revolution. They will be financially and legally supported by the state and federal governments and encouraged and supported by the state-sponsored media.

4. To institute programs and provide educational materials to all

state education systems, which will continue to create world citizens, and to instruct them in their role in the collective. In order to standardize these materials nationally, the Common Core has been developed.

a. To ensure that the populations remain submitted to the community *organizer* and the group of elite citizens who effectively provide for them.

b. To train students to be passionate about their community service and to instill their passion in others. This would operate exactly like passing down religious values from one generation to another. The common events and holidays that will unite the population would be those that advance the secular humanist agenda.

5. Ridicule and coercion may be used in order to protect the rights of the secular humanists and to silence those who would disrupt the community through contrary religious beliefs and traditional values.

6. To fully evaluate, infiltrate, and control all religious groups and organizations, inculcating these groups with the new thought and principles of religious secular humanism.

7. To elect to top leadership positions in any group, wherever possible, to be positioned to set policy, wherever possible, and eliminate the vestiges of traditional theism and institutionalize atheistic secular humanism.

8. To continue in unchecked control, the elite leadership will structure the social order so that there will never be peace, because continual unrest will ensure the need for an elite that is powerful and controlling. That there will always be social groups and classes that will be pitted against one another to ensure the unrest.

In 1933, as the first *Humanist Manifesto* was being penned, a great *difference* stood between the atheism of Friedrich Nietzsche and the atheism of the religious secular humanist. As we mentioned earlier, Nietzsche's atheism provided a certain dark hopelessness to the population who embraced it; however, the religious secular humanist is as passionate about his "religion" as any Christian of the day. He passionately desires to propagate his religion and passionately believes in its "replacement." Secular humanists provide for man's need for religion with their own brand of secular humanist religion. Their fervor is found in good works. We reiterate their motto: "Doing good without God." We will find the following text in the introduction to the second manifesto, which is to follow in this little book:

> Humanism can provide the purpose and inspiration that so many seek. It can give personal meaning and significance to human life.

This meaning and significance will be found in social organizations spearheaded by organizers around politics, the environment, and specific social change topics, such as sexual preference, feminism, self-actualization, and extreme sports. Each of these social change agents would bring about a sense of significance to their otherwise-meaningless human existence. All of them would be driven by political power. As each new humanist group is coalesced, they are given an enemy to fight and a war to win. The enemy is our traditional theist system. Hatred is aimed at theists, which can include Christians of any persuasion, Jews, Mormons, Seventh-Day Adventists, etc. Further, since the majority of Americans are White Anglo-Saxon Protestants, this creates a ready-to-use enemy for the movement to conquer. As long as there is an enemy, the revolution can advance. Following the introduction to *Humanist Manifesto II*, we will take a brief look at three of the impassioned political groups—specifically, the women's liberation or feminist movement, the controversy over Black and White race relations, or racism, and the embittered isolation and political activism of homosexuality.

CHAPTER 5

Humanist Manifesto II

This document was coauthored in 1973. Paul Kurtz was born in 1925 and is considered to be the primary influence. Kurtz is the former editor of *The Humanist* magazine and the father of modern humanism. He has also been a prominent plaintiff in several court cases that have established precedence to usher in humanist legal frameworks.

Included below is the preface for the manifesto. Following the preface and a brief rabbit trail where I will discuss my own perspective on some very hot-button issues that have been produced by national division, we will comb through the *Humanist Manifesto II*, taking one affirmation at a time to discern their effects on the United States social structure, law, and education. The preface is printed in its entirety, including the spelling and punctuation errors found in the published document. (Note that all italics are mine.)

Preface

It is forty years since *Humanist Manifesto I* (1933) appeared. Events since then make that earlier statement seem far too optimistic. Nazism has shown the depths of brutality of which humanity is capable. Other totalitarian regimes have suppressed human rights without ending poverty. Science has sometimes brought evil as well as good. Recent decades have shown that inhuman wars can be made in the name of peace. The beginnings of police states, even in democratic societies, widespread government espionage, and other abuses of power by military, political, and industrial elites, and the continuance of unyielding racism, all present a different and difficult social outlook. In various societies, the demands of women and minority groups for equal rights effectively challenge our generation.

As we approach the twenty-first century, however, an affirmative and hopeful vision is needed. Faith, commensurate with advancing knowledge, is also necessary. In the choice between despair and hope, humanists respond in the "*Humanist Manifesto II*" with a positive declaration for times of uncertainty.

As in 1933, humanists still believe that traditional theism, especially faith in the prayer hearing God, assumed to love and care for persons, to hear and understand their prayers and to be able to do something about them, is an unproved and outmoded faith. Salvationism, based on mere affirmation, still appears as harmful, diverting people with false hopes of heaven hereafter. Reasonable minds look to other means for survival.

Those who sign *Humanist Manifesto II* disclaim that they are setting forth a binding credo; their individual views would be stated in widely varying ways. This statement is, however, reaching for vision in a time that needs direction. It is social analysis in an effort to consensus. New statements should be developed to supersede this, but for today it is our conviction that humanism offers an alternative that can save present day needs and guide humankind toward the future.

The next century can and should be the humanistic century. Dramatic scientific, technological and ever-accelerating social and political changes crowd awareness. We have virtually conquered the planet, explored the moon overcome the natural limits of travel and communication: we stand at the dawn of a new age, ready to move farther into space and perhaps inhabit other planets. Using technology wisely, we can *control our environment, conquer poverty, markedly reduce disease, extend our lifespan, significantly modify our behavior, alter the course of human evolution and cultural development,* unlock vast new powers, and provide humankind with unparalleled opportunity for achieving an abundant and meaningful life.

The future is, however, filled with dangers. In learning to apply the scientific method to nature and human life, we have opened the door to ecological damage, overpopulation, dehumanizing institutions, totalitarian repression, and nuclear and biochemical disaster. Faced with apocalyptic prophesies and doomsday scenarios many flee in despair from reason and embrace irrational cults and theologies of withdrawal and retreat.

Traditional moral codes and newer irrational cults both fail to meet the pressing needs of today and tomorrow.

False "theologies of hope" and messianic ideologies substituting new dogmas for old, cannot cope with existing world realities. They separate rather than unite people.

Humanity, to survive, requires bold and daring measures. We need to extend the uses of scientific method, not renounce them, to fuse reason with compassion in order to build constructive social and moral values. Confronted by many possible futures we must decide which to pursue. The ultimate goal should be the fulfillment of the potential for growth in each human personality not for the favored few. But for all mankind *only a shared world and global measures will suffice.*

A humanist outlook will tap the creativity of each human being and provide the vision and courage for us to work together. This outlook emphasizes the role human beings can play in their own spheres of action. The decades ahead call for dedication, clear minded men and women able to marshal the will, intelligence, and cooperative skills for shaping a desirable future. Humanism can provide the purpose and inspiration that so many seek. It can give personal meaning and significance to human life.

Many kinds of humanism exist in the contemporary world. The varieties and emphasis of naturalistic humanism include "scientific", "ethical," "democratic," "religious," and "Marxist" humanism. Free thought, atheism, agnosticism, skepticism, deism, rationalism, ethical culture, and liberal religion all claim to be heir to the humanist tradition. Humanism traces its roots from ancient China, classical Greece and Rome, through the Renaissance and the Enlightenment, to

the scientific revolution of the modern world. But views that merely reject theism are not equivalent to humanism. They lack commitment to the positive belief in the possibilities of human progress and to the values central to it. Many within religious groups, believing in the future of humanism now claim humanist's credentials. Humanism is an ethical process through which we all can move above and beyond the divertive particulars, heroic personalities, dogmatic creeds, and ritual customs of past religions or their mere negations.

We affirm a set of common principles that can serve as a basis for united action—positive principles relevant to the present human condition. *They are a design for secular society on a planetary scale.*

For these reasons, we submit this new *Humanist Manifesto* for the future of humankind and for us, it is a vision of hope a direction for satisfying survival.

The passion that energizes such a revolution burgeons forth from well-meaning people with genuine fear for the future of mankind. The italicized portions in the preface may illustrate the compelling points that serve to keep those in the revolution tenaciously pressing on. The revolutionaries are fully convinced that they provide the greatest hope for the planet's survival. The change required is not optional; in fact, it's *demanded*. The foundation in the second *Humanist Manifesto* upon which the entire social structure must rest is summarized below:

1. Traditional theism is an unproved and out-moded faith that includes

   a. faith in the prayer-hearing God,
   b. the erroneous assumption that the prayer-hearing God loves and cares for you, and
   c. the erroneous assumption that the prayer-hearing God hears

and understands prayer.

2. Salvationism is harmful, as it ultimately will

   a. divert people from their work in life, and
   b. provide a false hope of heaven and the hereafter.

3. The next century can and should be the humanist century.

4. We should be able to

   a. control our environment,
   b. conquer poverty,
   c. markedly reduce disease,
   d. extend our life span,
   e. significantly modify our behavior, and
   f. alter the course of human evolution.

5. Traditional moral codes and newer irrational cults fail today's pressing needs and hope for the future. The following separate people:

   a. Theologies of hope
   b. Messianic ideologies

6. For humanity to survive, bold and daring measures must be taken.

Only a shared world and global measures will suffice. Humanism will bring all people together under one vision. It will

   a. organize people into a cooperative utilizing common skills to accomplish the stated goals, and
   b. establish a set of common principles as a set of basic action; these common principles will fuse reason and compassion.

7. The design is for a secular society on a planetary scale.

Now that we have a flavor of what will be tackled in the second manifesto, I would like to take the promised rabbit trail. You will note that one of the stated desires is to unite rather than to separate peoples. However, this new theology, which creates victims classes, has the effect of continuing to create division. The separation exists because of the group that they have identified rightly as people who believe in a prayer-hearing God who cares for them. It exists because these people believe that salvation and an eternal life are real and tangible. This can only describe Christianity and some Conservative, Bible-believing sects of Judaism.

Should you wonder why the social attack appears to be focused like a laser on the Christian community, and should it seem strange that the Christian communities in countries like Syria and Egypt receive little or no support from the United states, this preface from the second manifesto may provide you with insight. If you wonder why the media, on every level, use "born-again Christians" as the pariah to be scoffed at, derided, and belittled, this provides the answer. If you have wondered (as we did earlier) why the religion of Islam is greeted with open arms while Christianity is spurned, it is fully explained in a comprehensive reading of the preface of this document. In the Christian faith, including all the many different sects, you find a prayer-hearing God. All sects of the Christian belief system that embrace the God of the Bible believe in eternal life and the God that provides a way to that eternity. Most believe in the person of Jesus Christ, who is fully God and fully man, who has become the means to bridge the gap between God and man.

Secular humanists simply believe such a religion is "dangerous," and are attempting to rid this danger from our nation and the world in order to form a perfect secular state that will be instituted on a planetary scale and be able to meet all human problems into the future.

One might begin to believe that this war, which everyone senses is overtaking America—this Two Americas, as Mr. Edwards puts it— may not reflect the rich and the poor but rather the Judeo-Christian national roots and the secular humanists. Before we get to the heart of the document, it is prudent to consider three divisions in America that are used to create tension and division. To openly discuss my point of view regarding these politically correct divisions requires me to be both fearless and bold, because I believe it will open me up to mischaracterizations and false accusations. I do, however, believe it is time for a down-to-earth American to express their plain, simple values.

CHAPTER 6

A Brief Look at the Nation's Victim List

The divisions that the politicians would tell you make up the Two Americas would have to do with race, wealth, gender, and sexuality. A very personal look at these differences in America through my eyes will reveal why it is my contention that these separations are no more than devices to push the secular humanist agenda. I believe that the true divide in America today is between remaining a faithful theist who upholds the Founders' point of view or embracing the secular humanist worldview and helping to establish the national religion of atheism.

It is my strong belief that the accusation of racism, feminism, and homophobia all meet the desired level of attention to keep the proverbial eye off the real ball of intolerant secular humanism that divides us.

Utilizing these social groupings, citizens have been organized and manipulated into divisive and powerful groups. They are given media support, educational support, and congressional and court support. The groups are often formulated around legitimate complaints and grievances. The goal for the revolutionaries, however, is to use the people and organizations to create the illusion that these issues are the fundamental separation.

In fact, the true revolutionary does not want to solve the grievances or put away the structural complaints held by these three groups. This, to me, is smoke and mirrors. The humanist designers happily use these issues. They pit all groups against what used to be the primary cultural group of White Protestants. This tension will serve to work toward their ends. What follows is my personal view of these separate groups. I believe that my view may not be far from that of many of my fellow Americans; however, because I am about to speak very candidly and plainly, I would not be surprised if what I say will feed the flames of anger in several of these three groups.

The humanist elites who design and control victim groups will likely disagree with my perspective but may also disagree with my right to speak my opinion, but here goes. I want to address the feminist movement, Black relations in America, and the aggressive homosexual agenda from a nonintellectual White citizen's perspective.

The Feminist Movement

I attended university at the height of the feminist movement. My university was a very radical Northern California campus where, as I previously stated, they literally dismantled the economics department to free up funds for the feminist, Black, and Native American studies. The entire campus was steeped in feminism. Men were considered chauvinist pigs. Women ruled! Men had coerced and oppressed women in the prison called home and marriage, which ultimately enslaved them to the thankless task called homemaking. The new woman was one who would be free to realize her full potential and to embrace and enjoy her sexuality. Women were being challenged and prepared to take over every level of professional endeavor. Women were now going to be the competitor of men, not the complement to them. All distinctions between men and women were to be done away with. Women were no longer to be beside men as a companion—they were not even to be equal to men. Women were to become better than men, in every area, making men obsolete. I lived the process and the rhetoric of liberation and have now observed over these past forty years the actual results the liberation longed for.

I came from a home where my mother was the first woman in her family to graduate from high school, to move from her home to the big city to go to cosmetology school and graduate, and after a short time working for someone else, she opened her first of two beauty shops. These were all firsts in our immigrant family's life and were my proud heritage. I knew women were capable and smart. She was entirely successful, yet she gladly set it aside when my dad returned from the war in one piece and they decided to have a family. Throughout my childhood, she worked to add extra household income whenever she could. Dad helped with household chores, as did we kids, and we never thought of our mom as either enslaved or unequal. We were a family that worked and grew together. Dad had a place at the head of the house and the final word in any disagreement.

Back to the campus and 1972! The women's movement must have brought on a kind of euphoria for men. Men were no longer held responsible for women; there was no need for sexual fidelity or for the results of procreative behavior. They no longer paid for the dates. They were not expected to behave as gentlemen, nor were they put under the strain of growing up. These college lads had been dreaming about getting girls in their hands since their hormones were awakened when they were thirteen, but had been under the impression that a physical relationship implied responsibility. These lads (I can't bring myself to call them men) discovered through the feminist movement that their desires were to be met easily and with no required attachments. Most girls in my high school era, though sexually aroused and interested, were unwilling to run the risk of the loss of reputation or possible pregnancy for a fling. My peers still believed that sexuality was best inside the sacrament of marriage and with the promise of lifelong love and commitment. Their university indoctrination would change all that as the feminist movement took its toll.

The college boys woke up one day to the cry of feminism and freedom on campus. The next thing they knew, the girls were throwing away their bras along with their inhibitions. They were picking up free contraceptives, giddy on dope, and being instructed in their *university classrooms* that the morals of their parents were prudish and suffocating. The young men would no longer be required to treat women with respect, to court them, to be approved by their parents, or to work toward a meaningful career that could support a wife and family. The young men could move from one girl to another with impunity. The "boys" would not be required to grow into men. They could remain forever the irresponsible Peter Pan of the fairy tales. This is an exaggeration but still contains some amazing truth.

The women were being formally indoctrinated that having children was not as satisfying as having a career. We were taught that "bearing" children did not require raising children. We were instructed that a "woman needs a man like a fish needs a bicycle." No fathers needed, no marriage vows required! Children, who were inconvenient when conceived, were eliminated. Both men and women were delighted to be freed of the required responsibility of a child. The "free love" generation, it turned out, wasn't really loving, and the love expressed came at a high cost. It left scared, lonely lives scattered in every level of our society. The "free love" generation was really living out the humanistic worldview: all is material all the time and we must live for the day, for no eternity exists.

People, as it turned out, still yearned for commitment and moved into permanent relationships. My husband and I fell into that category. I will never forget when we conceived, I had old friends of mine ask me if we were going to "abort." I had never even considered such a thing, and it was here that my journey began in earnest to see feminism as a dark thief. In my mind the feminist thief deceived vulnerable, silly young men and women, stripping them of their dignity, of lifetime companionship, and of life's greatest joy, parenthood, and the challenge of raising and preparing children to be full adults in an ever-changing world.

As soon as I conceived, my entire body, mind, and spirit knew there was a child being formed. The mystery of actually carrying this amazing gift was the tonic that eventually turned my entire life into decades of joy. It was in this time of my life, too, that I had to wrestle with the reality of God. To be, in some strange sense, involved in His creation with this little person growing inside me was just breathtaking.

The feminist lie being fostered in classes, books, magazines, and popular TV was that women were enslaved and needed to be set free from traditional roles. The road to fulfillment was paved with sexual exploits and work outside the home. Competition with men should mean that women *will* rule. Men are only good for one thing, and that has nothing to do with either commitment or children. It was utterly clear to me that the university feminist rhetoric spoken as though it was a fact was, in truth, a hoax! Feminists spoke as though there was *nothing* left to be said! No reasonable person should debate the new truth that was unfolding. (Does *that* sound familiar? Think Al Gore and global warming.) This feminist movement was anything but "feminine," and while there were legitimate complaints that it was good to address, the underlying philosophy was humanism.

Women should be able to choose a workplace other than home, they should receive equal pay for their labors, and they should not have any man in a workplace treat them as an underling. Respect should be a part of every workplace. The men coming back from WWII were fully aware that it was the strength, courage, and ingenuity of the women at home that had built the machinery and kept both home and work going. The feminists took some areas that could legitimately be addressed and built them into a humanist social structure that attempts to remove the male-female differentiation found in the Judeo-Christian traditions, creation, and nature. The feminist movement was designed to institutionalize humanist values and silence traditional Judeo-Christian roles, morals, and institutions.

I was twenty-three at the time the feminist movement was taking the nation by storm and turning the culture on its head. I have since observed the results of feminism, and on the whole, I believe it has proved to be a wave of destruction in the individual lives of those who embraced it. It has formed a foundation of destruction for the traditional family. As a mother and as a professional for the past forty-five years, I have seen the difficulties of broken families and children raised by unmarried mothers with no masculine role models. I have seen incomes and retirement accounts divided because of divorce and am certain that this division of family resources has been one of the little-discussed elements of our nation's financial meltdown. The over-sixty crowd, trying to retire, is finding that the division of family resources due to divorces years past is affecting their retirement security. Many are left with little more than a Social Security check between them and homelessness. Mothers who left their children to be raised by others may be finding little to bind their children's affections to them as they are reaching their winter years, with little income and potentially failing health. The family unit was the target of the feminist movement.

The feminist movement attempted to convince the public that the role of the wife and mother was insignificant. The part of the discussion that was missing when I was in college was the complexity of the job of wife and mother. There was no acknowledgment of the intelligence, dedication, and wisdom that were required to be a support system to a husband and a trainer of the next generation. They did not mention that the mother was the heart of the home, nutritionist, nurse, economist, seamstress, judge, lawgiver, and teacher and that it was not just a job but a worthy and challenging calling.

The feminist movement indoctrinated an entire generation of men and women into the belief that the role of wife and homemaker was demeaning but that the challenge of bringing home the bacon was romantic and freeing. The feminist movement redefined the woman and her role in the family and, in so doing, moved the position of the man in the family to that of just another member of the team rather than the leader. The Judeo-Christian traditions require leadership of men. The feminists redesigned the family, thus eliminating the need for marriage and the requirement of a husband. Feminists degraded the most challenging and most important job in the world to meaningless slavery. The feminists are firmly attached to secular humanist principles. There is no God; we are material. The life we live is only for now, and one must accumulate as many events and as much excitement as possible. The feminists were dedicated pawns in the hands of the revolutionaries to institute the revolution of atheism. The extent that any thread of theism remains in the social fabric is proof of God's miraculous hand in lives of individuals. Secular humanists hate the concepts of guilt, shame, sin, and salvation and find those who rely on these truths to be a dangerous group.

The revolution remade the family. Feminists worked with religious zeal to recruit both women and men to their point of view. The school systems, beginning at the university level, were the purveyors of social change. They influenced instructors on their choice of books and the class requirements to ensure their point of view was exclusively taught.

The ultimate message to women was that the role of motherhood is irrelevant. The attendant message was that the role of a traditional wife not only was unimportant but was also slavery and a deterrent from a fulfilling life.

The feminists were convincing in their arguments to relinquish the responsibilities of motherhood. "If it feels good, do it" was a mantra that the professors were likely to teach. Situational ethics were taken to new heights. Money and influence were considered important. Faithfully taking up your role within the revolution to save the planet was an urgent and important goal.

Women, weary of the daily work at home, were ready to be important, so they headed off to university. I had many of these unhappy mothers in my classes. Like clockwork, the political structures grew government. They demanded increased taxes. Inflation occurred, and soon a household "required" two incomes to cover all their lifetime needs and hopes.

Concurrent with women returning to the university, bearing children outside of marriage no longer had a stigma attached to it. The federal government's programs were geared to reward those mothers who had neither husbands nor careers. There was a political agenda demanding the federal and state governments provide free day care so that married women would not be tied down to the house, and so that single mothers could provide for their children. This created the second greatest wave of women entering the workforce since 1942. As the role of government in the rearing of children grew, the role of God would diminish, thus fulfilling the humanists' ultimate goal of training a generation without the influence of the national Christian traditions. God was not considered as the ultimate provider in the lives of individuals through stable families. The government would, little by little, have a greater influence as provider for the American family. As we reach the virus crisis of 2020, we now see the government sending a check to every citizen. There was not a question of whether we had savings for such a time as this or if our families could take care of one another. No, the government stepped in as provider. This could be an ominous picture of things to come. I have worked some thirty years in an industry where I see the financial and life results of decisions made in concert with feminist indoctrination. I can truly say that what has been left in the wake of the feminist lie is both astonishing and sad. The women that have chosen to embrace lives outside traditional roles are frequently either divorced (sometimes several times) or alone. Many have been through numerous relationships and have no family history. I meet women my age who married, had children, and then with the encouragement of the feminist movement, left their marriage with the dream of a more perfect relationship. They are now, at sixty-plus, amazed that they never found anyone new and have no one who shares their history. Women that have lived in a monogamous, traditional, theist-driven marriage have been a vibrant part of the national workforce. They have been fulfilled in the roles as mothers and wives as well. These women who remained in traditional marriage (even if it was a second marriage) seem to me, anecdotally, to have more general happiness.

Ross Douthat, a *New York Times* columnist, wrote an article that seems to concur, and I have included a portion of that article below:

May 26, 2009
Op-Ed Columnist

Liberated and Unhappy Ross Douthat

American women are wealthier, healthier and better educated than they were 30 years ago. They're more likely to work outside the home, and more likely to earn salaries comparable to men's when they do. They can leave abusive and sue sexist employers. They enjoy unprecedented control over their own fertility. On some fronts—graduation rates, life expectancy and even job security—men look increasingly like the *second sex* [italics mine].

But all the achievements of the feminist era may have delivered women to greater unhappiness. In the 1960s, when Betty Friedan diagnosed her fellow wives and daughters as the victims of "the problem with no name," American women reported themselves happier, on average, than did men. Today, that gender gap has reversed. Male happiness has inched up, and female happiness has dropped. In postfeminist America, men are happier than women.

This is "The Paradox of Declining Female Happiness," the subject of a *provocative paper* [italics mine] from the economists Betsey Stevenson and Justin Wolfers. The paper is fascinating not only because of what it shows, but because the authors deliberately avoid floating an easy explanation for their data.

This column referring to the "happiness quotient" relevantly reflects on the feminist movement's influence on the way my generation and those following mine lived their lives. Many of us are increasingly attending memorial services these days, so we are acutely aware of the choices we have made. We traditionalists admit that our children and grandchildren are imperfect. Our marriages may be imperfect, but overall, we have a great deal of happiness in our traditional marriages and love the husbands who know and love us back. We glean love and respect from children and grandchildren. May I be so bold as to quote from Proverbs 31:28–31?

> Her children rise up and bless her; her husband also, and he praises her, saying: "Many daughters have done nobly, but you excel them all." Charm is deceitful and beauty is vain, but a woman who fears the Lord, she shall be praised. Give her the product of her hands and let her works praise her in the gates.

As it turns out, Proverbs 31, this biblical picture of the model woman, describes the facets of the life of a woman who "did it all." This woman took care of the home and the finances, planned for the retirement, took care of directing her servants, made and sold items, was a real estate genius who bought and sold land, and many more things. But she was, first and foremost, a wife and mother, dedicated to her own household. I think that it is truly the very picture of a fulfilled woman, but then this Proverbs 31 woman would not fit the secular humanist parameters and so must be destroyed!

We would be remiss to discuss the feminist movement without including the fact that the wide availability of free or inexpensive contraception, which block conception, and the legalization of abortion, up until the time the child is naturally born, has served as its bedrock philosophy. The sexualization of society, and certainly of children, has taken place as an expression of the feminist movement. The true feminist dogma, as long as pregnancy could be avoided or terminated, had no moral parameters, no age limits, and no constraints in regard to marriage vows.

The "war on women" that has been falsely created over this past election cycle has far less to do with women's rights than the freedom of religion secured by our First Amendment.

The feminist agenda, in the end, has had much more to do with establishing the humanist agenda and the breakdown of traditional family in America than it has the freedom of women to blossom, succeed, and have a rich and fulfilling life.

So to reiterate, the feminist movement has been used by the humanists. Some women join me in believing that while there were some legitimate issues to address, overall, the movement was a sham used to divide men and women and allocate political power to humanist politicians who are bringing about the revolution. Many of the women who swallowed the whole lie have reviewed their "freedom" with some sorrow:

1. Some women my age are poor and alone. Some left stable but imperfect marriages to find that life was difficult and not what they had anticipated.

2. The women who embraced a lifestyle without children find that they are nearing an end of life without the joy and hope of a new generation in their lives.

3. The feminists who swallowed the entire lie about men have lived in a prickly independence and may have missed the joy of having a man actually care for them, understand their needs, travel through life with them, and hold their history in his hands.

4. Some women discovered too late that going to work wasn't as glamorous as the leaders of the women's liberation movement promised. They found that their freedom from home was a lifetime of slavery to a paycheck.

5. Some who had children alone did fine; many have not done well, and the fruit of the mothering, which was portrayed as inconsequential, is noticeable in the character, or lack thereof,

of their grown children.

What were some of the consequences to men?

1. Women who once held a role of encouraging and building men up were now competitors. Men were belittled, and their importance as men was questioned.

2. Men were no longer required to make a commitment. The act of committing to a woman, to care for her and raise a family, is often the single most important act in a man's life. This very act of commitment redirects the *selfish* boy to a life path of a *selfless* man. The man that is able to lead a family becomes a part of the societal fabric as a whole. They have an investment in their children and the world around them. This selfless role challenges everything that is natural to a man's makeup, so God, in His wisdom, asks the man to be selfless.

3. Some men abdicated leadership and took on a more subservient role in the house. This feminization of young men has made them indecisive, unmotivated, and childish, not to mention less attractive!

4. If nothing noble is required of men, then the great quality of selfless love necessary in a father and husband would no longer be expected. Again, let me be so bold as to quote a scripture that is applicable here and certainly would be hated by the secular humanists:

> Husbands love your wives as Christ loved the church and gave Himself for her. (Eph. 5:25)

For theists, this instruction from God poses a great challenge. It challenges his very selfish nature. For the atheist, it is foolish, for it assumes a god who cares for the individual.

1. Men have been debilitated and humiliated so that unless they are still raised in a traditional theist home and church setting, they likely no longer see themselves as protector and provider. The social structure has changed over the years to support a feminist point of view.

2. We own an apartment complex. We have more unwed parents than married parents who apply. We had one couple live at the apartment for five years. They were a lovely Hispanic couple with four adorable children. While I know that family and faith are often important to the Hispanic population, this couple would not marry and the children were growing up in a household with a man who refused to marry their mother. A marriage would have caused them to lose her government subsidy. Eventually, the man of the family left, and the young woman is now raising the children alone.

3. Divorce and failure to marry create a situation where children bounce from home to home, like lost puppies. The state makes decisions regarding where the children will live. The state oftentimes feeds and houses the unwed mother while her "significant other" lives in the house without legal responsibility for anyone.

4. This new social order sprung from feminism. The redefinition of the woman's role and of the family were the perfect starting place for destroying the vestiges of the Founders' Judeo-Christian worldview. It served to establish humanism as the social structure, atheism as the national religion, and government as the elite structure to redistribute wealth and services.

I fail to see a winner that has emerged from the feminist movement. I call it the feminist folly. The women have lost their mystery and deep feminism, and the men remain little boys, to be cared for, rather than grow into men who care for others. The humanists desire this coalition of women to remain as part of their political divisions. They are still able to use the feminists' role models to coalesce votes based on fear of the rights of abortion to change or fear of loss of birth control. The true grievance of workplace equality in respect and pay was met a very, very long time ago, but the revolutionists must continue to use this well-worn philosophy to divide the nation, because to admit to the value of the traditional family or the traditional role of the woman would be to bow to the possibility that a theistic view of life and corporate national life may have a place left in America.

Black Relations and the Charge of Racism

At the time of this writing, the Black Lives Matter movement has exploded in the city streets, on basketball courts, on football fields. The demand for people to bend the knee and profess that "Black lives matter" is now rampant.

With that being acknowledged, I believe that what I have to say on this subject could be said by millions of Americans but sadly never is! Public figures who make accusatory and false statements about my feelings (grouping all White people) against Black people are infuriating.

Public figures often presume that if I hold a certain point of view, I am racist. I have never lived in an inner city, nor have many millions of others. I have also never lived in a mansion. I have never lived in New York or LA, nor have I lived in the South. When I hear a speaker gather all "White people" into one convenient group and accuse them of racism while proclaiming the privileges that they have had in being White, I consider them preposterous. The assumption that if you are White you are born with a silver spoon in your mouth, that jobs are automatically handed to you, that money jumps into your bank account, and that influence is automatic is utter nonsense. The person that would say such a thing is either entirely ignorant regarding White culture or intends to create division rather than unity. I scoff at his foolish, naive speech and can only hope that his audience is not so uninformed as to believe him or be manipulated by him. These deceptive leaders have wielded their influence and speaking ability to stir up division, covetousness, and bitterness and to maintain a fire of animosity here in the United States that needs to be addressed and healed.

We each have a life. It has a beginning and an ending. Our lives have influences, some good and some bad. We each have certain restrictions. We can have financial restrictions, health and physical limitations, mental strengths and weaknesses. We each have circumstances, people, and ideas that influence our lives. The influential people can be parents, teachers, extended family, pastors, or gang leaders. The circumstances can be wealth or poverty, parents or no parents. We can have parents who are wise in their discipline yet either physically or mentally absent. We can have parents who work or are lazy. There are parents of all colors who are addicted to alcohol and some that entirely abstain from alcohol. We each have a heritage of nationality, physical, mental, and spiritual features; we are born to a socioeconomic level, and we have educational opportunities and limitations. Contrary to the secular humanists who think in terms of groups, we are not a collective separated into groups that are opposing one another and vying for finite resources. The biblical worldview sees the individual; we are not a collection of White, another collection of Black, another collection of Yellow, and still another Brown. We are not a collection of women or of men or of gays and straights. We are individuals. It is very offensive and foolish for a TV talking head, or a spokesman from a group, or a journalist from the mass media, to use their public position to accuse millions of people at a time of racism. Equally offensive is the assumption that all White people, because of a specific point of view, are racist. I am, at my core, a Capitalist. This core belief does not make me a racist. I want an opportunity for all who will work to succeed. Color means absolutely nothing to me or, frankly, to anyone I have ever known. I deeply resent the media and public figures for not being honest about the racial tensions in our country. It is time to admit that much of the tension is *created* and kept alive and well by the revolutionaries. We need to acknowledge that there have been governmental policies that have isolated Black communities by removing fathers, not encouraging families, providing poor educational opportunities by keeping "choice" from those neighborhoods. The humanist ideal is to identify victims held captive to

Capitalism or traditional values and exploit them for the express desire of national turmoil and judicial change. This turmoil is necessitated by the revolutionaries, whose goal it is to destroy the foundational governing principles of theism, free enterprise, and national sovereignty. The end to this destruction is that Socialism, atheism, and one-world governance replace our original system. I further resent feeling like I must watch what I do or say about the Black community, lest someone think I am a racist. When I was a child—and now as an adult—I loved to read. I would empathetically enter into the lives of other people of various races, cultures, and historic periods through biographies and autobiographies. I have wept at the suffering of Anne Frank and Corrie ten Boom. I have also wept at the lives of slaves that were tortured and sold. I was horrified by the injustice suffered by families that were separated or women who worked in mansions and were used as mistresses. I have traveled the backwoods and rivers alongside Lewis and Clark and met the beautiful Sacagawea in pages of precious books. I have read much on the Civil War and the civil rights movement and felt the indignation of the people sent to the back of the bus, and shame for the White people that did such evil things. I like to think I would have done everything possible to free the slaves or to create a social structure where everyone was equally honored had I been present at the time those battles were being fought.

The fact remains that I lived through the events of my life and you have lived through the events of *yours*. I am convinced that the hardships and limitations of one's life are not nearly as debilitating as the wrong reaction to those hardships and limitations. I did not grow up in a Black community or an inner city, but my lack of experience with that world must not presume that I have a racist cell in my body. I do not believe that I do. If I stare at Black people when I am in the room with them, it is because I think the very nature of their rich, clear skin is uniquely beautiful. I stare at Black people sometimes simply because I am outside of their culture, and my stare is as one outside of a window looking in to partake and understand. I am struck by the magnificence of the Creator's touch in the beauty of the skin, the eyes, and the noble profiles one sees in the Black community. I am guilty of doing the very same thing when I am in a group of Mexican Americans, Iranians, or Indians—each ethnic group has a particular beauty. The shades of skin, genetic shapes, and facial features that may be common to a given group all serve as a reminder of God's great creative genius.

We lived on Air Force bases in noncommissioned-officer housing when I was young. Color was never an issue. We played with the kids on the block. We laughed and appreciated one another. We had common values, such as, we didn't steal, we didn't lie, we didn't treat one another terribly, and we were patriotic and went to parades where great music was played. We had an overwhelming pride when we saw the Thunderbirds perform or the flag waving. We exuberantly sang patriotic songs at school. We sang Christmas songs together, and we had pageants at Christmas and Mayday and did Easter egg hunts together. We seemed like an enormous quilt, different fabric put together in some carefully designed pattern to make up life— wonderful life. We were fair to one another but never failed to be competitive. We fought to win at baseball, skating, jacks, marbles, racing, dodgeball, and tetherball. Some won all the time, and others weren't necessarily the winners, but we liked one another and were glad for anyone who won and were not cruel to those who did not.

There was the normal "cruelty" of the child's life where some would call others' names. There was some bullying; we didn't all agree, but this childish cruelty was not along black-and-white lines. I remember both Black and White boys and girls exceeding my popularity. They were cool and admired. We would never think to call a Black friend by some derogatory name, and likewise, I do not believe they thought to accuse us of racism. If we beat them at competition, we were not racists; we were the winners. My parents invited the neighbors over for barbeque. If they were White, they were invited; if they were Black, they were invited. Black and White skin never determined planning or outcomes of events.

Even as a child, I would look into the face of my Black neighbors and think that their smile seemed more fetching than mine, and their music was different from the country Western and big band played at our house. Their family was fun and seemed close.

Those are my memories of Color in my childhood. There was a difference in color, but the difference was interesting and beautiful. There was a difference in cultural heritage, but the difference was interesting and fun and made life fuller. In all, people were *not the same*; they were *different*. I was different. And I am still different! All to the glory of a creative God! I wonder how many of my dear readers would say they are as well, and vive la différence!

When I got to high school, I was in a big city. There were some gangs, and drug use was beginning to be widespread. I would see tough-looking gangs and really did not care if they were White, Mexican, or Black—I was terrified because they were crude and violent. They did not share my values. I was not racist, but I did not want to be anywhere near them. The color meant nothing to me, but their *behavior* and their *values* were foreign. I deplored their coarseness. Any "me and them" sprung not from prejudice toward skin color but because unlike my childhood friends, who were fair, conscientious, humorous, kind, and mostly openly God-fearing, these people were crude and uncivilized. They used horrible language and seemed evil and mean. Their style was to dress, speak, and act in an aggressive, belligerent manner.

Our family may not have been considered middle class. We never lived in a home my parents owned until I was a junior in high school. We were tenants of small homes in common neighborhoods. We did not think of ourselves as above anyone but oddly never felt below anyone. We just were; we were exactly who we were. We had some academic strength, a good sense of humor, an enjoyment for life. We were very *imperfect* kids with very imperfect parents. By the time we were young teens, we knew we would have to work to earn the money to get along. I can't remember having had this said to me, but I knew it. It was my responsibility to be a productive citizen. That being said, we began our working career mowing lawns and babysitting at age twelve. By age sixteen, I worked part-time at a hospital and moved into full-time work in the summer.

It was not until my college years that racism became known to me. The sixties brought awareness of the racial inequality that still existed. It was then that I began to be aware that our laws did not provide equality for all. I did not feel differently toward people of different color than myself, but I started thinking I must bend over backward to repay the Black Americans for the sins of my grandfather, and those of his grandfather before him. It was likely 1969 before I listened to and agreed with Dr. Martin Luther King's speech, which instructed us that "people be judged by the content of their character, not the color of their skin." By the time I heard this speech, this lovely man had been assassinated. College courses began to alter my childhood awareness, and the suffering of the Black community became a concern. It would be many years before I began to grasp how the demonic hand of slavery had altered the history of the whole world. In fact, slavery was certainly not unique to America. However, it was America's uniquely Christian underpinnings that made it the single most destructive policy in our nation's history. Slavery is the antithesis of the freedom that is promised in our founding documents. Unfortunately, if we do not stop the humanistic control over our nation, these documents will be undone and we will become slaves to the state. If the revolutionaries complete their plan, a small, all-powerful elite government will become "god," and the citizens their slaves.

I believe that the enslavement of other human beings was so inconsistent with the personal faith of individual citizens that eventually grief of this practice created the courage to fight the powerful culture of slavery, which was tied into the South's economic success and comfort. The power of conviction fueled the fire that led men, women, and families to pay for this horrible national sin by shedding blood and spending treasure in great quantities to purchase the freedom of the Black person in America.

The next stage of the Black man's struggle was for equality of vote, enjoyment of personal success, and equal honor. These have been slower to come. The meanness of man's spirit desires to have someone below him so that he may have dominance. This battle would be fought on many levels as the Black citizens struggled for their equal footing. I had not perceived prejudice as a child, but it was there. The sixties began to set into law equality of rights. It was sorely needed. No more redlining mortgages, no more HOAs that said Black people could not live there, and no separate schools and water fountains.

Because of man's heart, not all are now colorblind; however, as an adult, I truly cannot remember anyone who has ever said anything against someone because of the color of their skin. I cannot remember anyone not being welcomed because of the color of their skin. I am not so naive as to think that this does not exist, yet it appears that it is rather rare and isolated.

So the question would exist: Are there people I do avoid? The answer is a resounding yes! I still avoid the crude, the mean, the brash, or the seemingly violent, unless I feel that I can both serve them and draw them nearer to God, who would bring light into their lives.

Dr. Martin Luther King's words still ring true: "It is the content of their character, not the color of their skin," by which a man should be judged.

Politically, however, the Black community is used in the war against our heritage by the secular humanists. The humanist design is to bring about strife, division, and dependence. They have been able to isolate the Black community in such a way as to advance the themes of situational ethics, destruction of the family unit, and redefinition of the role of the man in a family. They have used covetousness as a theme, and inequality of goods to create an ongoing strife and division. These humanists, who love and employ strife between groups, have kept the Black population as victims. Through the inequality argument, they are able to set the stage for the worldwide redistribution of wealth and Socialism.

A proof of the way the Black community is manipulated is best seen in a chart of "Whiteness" that was found in the National Museum of African American History and Culture in Washington, DC. I was made aware of this chart in a *Washington Examiner* "Opinion" article by Becket Adams on July 15, 2020, the stated goal is for the black American to reject "white qualities."

He included the chart, which I have included below. The comments that follow are mine.

"The "White Qualities" on the sign read as follows:

TALKING ABOUT RACE NMAAHC

Aspects &Assumptions of **Whiteness** &
White Culture in the United States

White dominant culture or **whiteness**, refers to the ways white people and their traditions, attitudes and ways of life have been normalized over time and are now considered standard practices in the United States. And since white people still hold more of the institutional power in America, we have all internalized some aspects of white culture-including people of color.

Rugged Individualism:	The individual is the primary unit—Self reliance Independence & autonomy highly valued + rewarded Individuals assumed to be in control of their environment, You get what you deserve
Family Structure:	The nuclear family: father, mother, 2.3 children as ideal social unit Husband is breadwinner and head of household Wife is homemaker and subordinate to the husband Children should have own rooms, be independent

History: Based on Northern European immigrants' experience in the U.S.
Heavy focus on the British Empire
The primacy of Western (Greek, Roman) and Judeo Christian tradition

Protestant Work Ethic: Hard work is the key to success
Work before play
If you didn't meet your goals, you didn't work hard enough

Religion: Christianity is the norm
Anything other than Judeo-Christian tradition is foreign
No tolerance for deviation from single god concept

Status, Power and Authority: Wealth= worth
Your Job is who you are Respect authority
Heavy value on ownership of goods, space and property

Future Orientation: Plan for future—delayed gratification
Progress is always best......... "Tomorrow will be better"

Time: Follow rigid time schedules—Time viewed as a commodity

Aesthetics:	Based on European culture—steak and potatoes; "bland is best" Woman's beauty based on blonde, thin "Barbie" Man's attractiveness based on economic power, intellect
Holidays:	Based on Christian religions Based on white history and male leaders
Justice:	Based on English common law Protect property and entitlements Intent counts
Competition:	Be #1 Win at all costs Winner/loser dichotomy Action Oriented Master and control nature Must always "do something" about a situation Aggressiveness and Extroversion Decision-making Majority rules (when whites have power)
Communications:	"The King's English" rules Written tradition Avoid conflict, intimacy Don't show emotion Don't discus personal life Be Polite

"Whiteness," reads the headline to a museum webpage dedicated specifically to the organization's efforts to explain White people. "Since White people in America hold most of the political, institutional, and economic power, they receive advantages that non-White groups do not."

You know, this does not get better from here, right?

The Smithsonian webpage, which is maintained by the federal government, includes an astonishingly racist graphic titled, "Aspects and Assumptions of Whiteness and White Culture in the United States."

These "aspects and assumptions" include but are not limited to rugged individualism, respect for authority, being polite, and even punctuality. The graphic continues, claiming that White people place a premium on hard work, competitive drive, the nuclear family, objectivity, the scientific method, self-reliance, and hope.

The obvious implication here is that non-Whites (Blacks, Latinos, Asians, and others) are monolithic, lawless, impolite, selfish, lazy, apathetic, irrational, backward, dependent, and hopeless.

They need to shun Christianity and the core traditional family. That is not who the Black people are in America, yet those who desire to divide in order to conquer our culture evidently desire to cast them as such for their own ends.

I am reminded of a quote from Thomas A. Edison, who said, "I have friends in overalls whose friendship I would not swap for the favor of the kings of the world." I suspect that this expresses how most of us feel. We form kinships with people, not on their wealth, but on their personal qualities that are attractive to us. It has brought grief to have created this "Black victim" class within our society. It has spurred the division we see today. If we can turn the head of this dragon called humanism, we can gain honor for all.

It is the politicians and certain members of the media that seem to have a whip on all our backs, continuing to fan any old flames of racism that remain, with an attempt to paint with a broad brush any disagreement of a lifestyle with an animosity toward a race. The incident with Trayvon Martin and George Zimmerman was utilized to separate, destroy, and encourage race as a division by our previous president. It was interesting to note that during the same time, Antonio Santiago, a thirteen-month-old White child, was shot point-blank by two young Black men and murdered for no reason. It received no news. When the seventeen-year-old De Marquise Elkins was charged with the murder of Antonio and the fourteen-year-old, whose name was never released, was also charged, there was some local coverage, but nothing further. There is no national coverage for the hundreds of Black-on-Black crimes that happen every year in our major American cities, nor is there national attention given to the hundreds of Black-on-White crimes committed. This deplorable incident, which President Obama used to further the racial division, while unfortunate, should not have sparked the aftermath that occurred, except it was used by media and politicians.

In 2020, we are dealing with the aftermath of a terrible public killing of a Black man, George Floyd, by a police officer. This horrendous and public killing has been used for one purpose—to create the ongoing breakdown in the social fabric that will allow for government to have a still-greater role in our lives, which the humanist agenda demands.

There is no one of any color that would suggest that this killing was justified. We must consider that the level of looting, rioting, destruction, beatings, and even killings which have erupted from this one act is the very picture of the humanist agenda being thrust upon the entire nation, with the result that we are more divided than we have ever been. I, for one, am just done with even listening to it. The accusations, the stirring up of strife, and the planting of bitter roots throughout the community and the nation through well-designed media attention are a methodology exercised to exacerbate any residual racial divisions. But, make no mistake, race is not the division that forms the Two Americas. It is being used to destroy the Founders' principles and replace them with a secular society that relinquishes our sovereignty and gives way to an elite power that will redistribute all wealth and goods according to their own design.

The past is over. The future lies ahead. We treat one another with respect and fairness but need not attempt some backward contortion just because someone is another color, nor is it possible to make up for the past. We forgive and move forward. It is each person's responsibility to stand up, take ahold of life, and live it. If I were a whiner, I could whine all day about going to so many schools, having all sorts of different schooling methods, having no roots either in the community or with people. I chose at some point to consider that all my background gave me strength and insight for my life. So it is with a Black person, a Yellow person, an Italian—oh yes, that's me! In the end, it is personal values (which include spiritual beliefs) that are the glue to bring a community together or to divide it, not color or sex or nationality. Camaraderie is built on fundamentals that exceed the cost of the blouse you wear, the income tax that you pay, the car that you drive, the neighborhood that you live in, or the color of your hair or eyes. It far exceeds the school you attended or whether you were the class cheerleader or a wallflower. Those public figures who use speech with the goal of division are certain to be secular humanists functioning in accordance with their directive documents.

Unity occurs when there are shared values and mutual respect for the part the individual plays in life. The shared values of love of God, coupled with absolute values of truthfulness, diligence, thoughtfulness, selflessness, loyalty, fidelity, thriftiness, and mutual respect of each person's abilities, are the glue that holds us together and makes us strong. Sharing the same financial position does nothing to formulate a kinship or friendship. Once again, I will say that those public figures who disdain financially successful people do so to cause covetousness and divide and pit groups against one another for one purpose and one purpose only: they desire to have the power to control all wealth and redistribute it according to their purposes.

I have a business that sometimes requires the work of a locksmith. I remember telling him one day, "I don't know what I would do without you here. You may not think you perform a huge service, but when I need to have new locks, I would not know where to turn without you. You are so diligent. Thank you!" He seemed shocked to hear my heartfelt praise. If you want to know his color so you can put that little interchange into a box, just call him Green. Most people do not think about color in their interactions with others. We learn to know people with skills, personalities, intelligence, and moral values. Another book could be written for me to express both the wrongs of the past as well as the wrong methods we have instituted to make corrections. But suffice it to say that my personal test of what I have said about Black and White relations came when my precious and beautiful eldest daughter came home from high school and asked me what I thought about her going out with a Black boy. My response to her is one I still believe to be my guiding truth and would mirror many people's truth. I said I did not care what color his skin was—I wanted to know who his parents were. I wanted to know if they were Christians, if they were honorable in their work. I wanted to know if he was an honest young man and if he strove to be a good student, with a clear goal set for excellence in all that he did. Did he honor his parents, his teachers, and his classmates? Did his language represent a good vocabulary, or was he mired in slang and profanity? I would have said the same thing about a boy she was interested in that was White.

Those are still my criteria—the heart of the person, their diligence, their inner strength, and their personal qualities are the scale we should all use to measure the person that would spend time with our daughters. The color of their skin is a part of their personal beauty, not an indication of social class.

Sometime after my daughter was grown and married, she moved to St. Louis, Missouri, into a small suburb. The neighborhood was a mixture of Black, White, and East Indian. The community, as a whole, was much more eclectic than the neighborhood she grew up in. She had an experience that shook her to the core and will remain with her forever. Her next door neighbors had a darling little three-year-old daughter. She saw her out in front and said, "Hi, honey, how old are you?" The little girl began to cuss her out with words that befitted a gang member, not a little girl. The child called her all sorts of horrible names and did so with hatred in her voice. My daughter was shaken and called me to tell me about the event. She conveyed the anger this little child spoke with and was almost in shock that someone could impart such a deep hatred to such a young child. I said,

"Honey, you have just seen the face of racism." These people are training their children in hatred and violence against White people as a group. I warned her not to allow the experience with this one racist family to make her assume that all the people in that group were alike. Her time in Missouri also revealed some White people that were equally ugly and racist.

As it turned out, she worked with people of different colors and ethnicities that year. Most were wonderful; some were individually racist, but oddly enough, most of the racism she encountered was from individual Black people toward White. She confirmed that all White people were not a certain way, all Indian people did not fall into a category, and certainly, all Black people did not fall into a category. They were each individual. The revolutionaries must have us in categories in order to create division and realize their political goals. When we hear speakers who refer to Americans coupled with some absurd accusation of racism, it is wise to consider that they may be secular humanist revolutionaries attempting to break down the social fabric. Those people who attempt to make political policy and formulate dependent groups of individuals, pitting one group against another, ultimately desire to break down individualism and move all citizens toward a controllable collective. They would not be able to conquer the entire social structure unless the citizenry is kept busy in shadow battles against one another.

A national policy that reflects our Founders' view would never advocate single parenthood or a social structure where parents are removed from the responsibility of the training, feeding, and caring of their own children. Our social policies should work to deliver any person from government interference. The secular humanist methodology is to institute public policy and train public thinking which has, at its core, the concept of rights and demands and which envisions government as provider rather than the presumption of personal responsibility.

The result of a social construct where individuals are raised with a victim mentality and fed with lies about the privilege and wealth of other social groups is deeply flawed, false, and destructive. To be trained on a belief that gain will come as a result of demanding rights is, at its core, unwise and contrary to our Founders' philosophy. Social policy built on humanist theology will ultimately fail to free people or to grant the equal outcomes promised. The final outcome of such humanist policies will be two classes. There will be the ruling elite, who have no limit to their powers. They will dole out to the pitiful, dependent servant class the portion they believe is just, of the world's goods. The public assertion of racism, coupled with the group indoctrination into rights and unearned privilege, will assure division, contention, and a certain mental slavery. Should the revolutionaries continue this strategy of divide and conquer, they will succeed in creating an angry and bitter populace. They will one day completely destroy the family unit, as pictured by the theistic founders and proved as an effective social foundation. This applies to Black, Brown, and White and Italian, French, English, and Polish— all colors and ethnicities alike. Our social rules and expectations should not need to be altered because of someone's race or skin tone. We should never need to accept one-parent households, lack of academic success, enslavement to government handouts for one group over another—that *would* be racist!

I believe many people, Black and White alike, share my feelings in this, but until we speak up and strip the secular humanists of their power to divide us into warring groups, we will continue to hear the term racist used as a blanket of derision covering our population and dividing us. I know the Black/White issue can have many more complications; however, the simplicity of allowing butterflies to struggle forth from the cocoon where they have metamorphosed leads one to conclude that each individual must make the best of their own circumstances. Life is absolutely *not* a group sport; it is an individual race.

We should not excuse away behaviors that are utterly destructive or incompetent just because the persons doing them are Black or Brown or White—that *would* be racist.

The secular humanist revolutionaries who pit Black against White or Mexican American against White or Black desire to eliminate the individual and deal with collectives. They speak in terms of the collective. This is a divisive philosophy used for the purpose of bringing about the revolution.

These revolutionaries are now applying all the same tactics to the Hispanic Americans and using illegal immigration as another great tool of division. I believe most Americans do not have any ill feelings toward Hispanics. I love them and their culture. What is of concern is the ongoing designed incompetence of our government to simply stop the influx of illegal immigrants of all nationalities by exercising the current laws. This topic is of great use for the secular humanists because it not only creates division but also opens the floodgate to destroy our national sovereignty. The humanists believe that America must lose her borders to become part of the designed one-world government.

The immigration "crisis," like many of the politically designed crises, is simple. Anyone who comes out of the shadows and has a proved residence for more than five years, who has been self-supporting with no public aid and no arrests, should be granted citizenship without the right to vote. The right to vote can be granted to their children. A person granted their citizenship but withholding the right to vote would have a different-colored driver's license. Those who do not meet this criterion should, without question, be put on transportation to the capital city of their nation of origin. People from other countries should be able to work here with a green card but not receive public assistance and not in the area of employment where Americans are available to fill those positions. People who have applied for legal citizenship should not be held up for years on end but given clear consideration and moved along in the legal immigration process. All people who immigrate to our country should learn our English so that they can integrate into our culture, business, and social structure. In addition, they need to have classes in history and economics. Our strong will to close the borders should be exercised. Now that I have "ruffled feathers" with my views about feminism, the Black-White relations, and possibly my illegal immigrant policies, I want to make a statement about homosexuals and the homosexual movement in America, which may call for me to be tarred and feathered!

Homosexuality vs. the Homosexual Political Movement

In order to grasp the politically aggressive homosexual movement, we must look at the social change agent of this political movement completely outside of the context of homosexuality as a sexual preference.

Because we are systematically being silenced, I am going to posit something that might be seen as politically incorrect, but I believe I speak for many traditionally thinking Americans when I say that there is nothing new under the sun. Homosexuality has always been present. It is part of every age, and likely every culture. It is and has always been present in every level of every society, high, low, rich, poor, cultured, uncultured. One will find people with homosexual desires in the clergy, in the teaching profession, as ditchdiggers, politicians, and military personnel. Any adult knows this. Perhaps the most deeply affected by someone living out a homosexual or lesbian lifestyle are the family members and friends of those of this preference.

The great difference about homosexuality in our current culture is that this lifestyle has been co-opted by secular humanists as a political tool. It was determined that this particular "victim group" could be used to completely undermine Judeo-Christian roots and presence in society. Ultimately, this group has aggressively used the courts and legislatures to amass more rights and freedoms, often at the cost of the basic religious freedoms that are granted in the Bill of Rights. As the court cases are handed down and law is formed, it will ultimately either grant the homosexual rights pre-eminence or allow freedom of religion to stand. At present, when the two freedoms are pitted against each other, the LGBT rights win out.

Several years ago, there was a great Chick-fil-A controversy that sent the political side of the LGBT community into a battle with this company. The owner of the company made a comment that he supported the traditional view of marriage. He is openly a confessing Christian, so his view should not have come as a surprise, but it exploded in the media like a literal bombshell. Watching this battle unfold brought clarity to my mind regarding this social phenomenon like no other single event.

The owner was very well-spoken, not hateful or mean, but expressed his personal opinion for traditional marriage and was literally almost crucified for his position. The intolerant gay activist community, in concert with the secular humanist media, attempted to use his comments to destroy him, his business, and anyone who was associated with the business. The intolerant governmental change agents in various cities revealed the plan that will be implemented lest we get this secular humanist revolution stopped. They rose up with governmental power and absolute authority as to whether they would allow a Chick-fil-A, a private business, to remain in their community because of the personal views of the owner. To retain a personal belief that marriage is defined as one man and one woman was considered politically incorrect and potentially affected his business's worthiness. It appears that the unpardonable sin is to hold to traditional values. To suggest that people who have a preference for the same sex should not have the privilege of redefining the union of marriage, which has been held for thousands of years and is fundamental to our social structure, is portrayed as a crime.

There is no question that we have same-sex couples as part of our current social structure, but in a "free" country, one should have the right to believe that the marriage union is reserved for one man and one woman. When that *freedom* of thought and expression is taken and the right to own a business is stripped because of that freedom of thought, we will have turned a corner and lost ground we may never be able to regain.

The Supreme Court of the land made a decision this year that supports LBGT rights over those of people of faith. It is undeniable that same-sex marriage and homosexual privilege over traditional citizens are a perfect political vehicle for this revolution. When this one sweeping change is completed, an unmovable intolerance will clutch this nation to the end, that those who hold traditional biblical views will not only be silenced but will also be threatened with the force of law if they dare to pass on their firmly held religious beliefs to their children.

Since the revolutionaries continually seek an opportunity to destroy current traditional thought, at the same time weakening the generational attachment to Judeo-Christian values and beliefs, this is the perfect venue to accomplish both. The owner of the Chick-fil-A Corporation was not intolerant of homosexuality, nor was he hateful to individual homosexual people. He made a statement of his fealty to traditional beliefs and traditional marriage. This fanned outrage by the media and outrage by the gay community. One gay man in our community of Tucson thought it appropriate to spew his outrage at a sweet girl hired to take and provide his order at Chick-fil-A. The change agent revolutionaries, in concert with their voice, the public media, were happy to deny the Capitalist his right to speech and right to personal opinion. I believe that those people who denied him his opinion and ability to express his view are the ones that are entirely intolerant. The gay activist's movement is intolerant. I hope I am correct in believing that not all individual homosexual people agreed with this outrage. I can only hope that as individual Americans, they desire that their fellow businessmen and fellow Americans have every right to express their personal preference for traditional marriage.

Our quiet public response to the Chick-fil-A incident was interesting and went unrecognized by the media that had tried to destroy the corporate owner. The public went out in droves to Chick-fil-A to eat! All over the country, people who had never entered this restaurant went for lunch and dinner.

This attack against businesses that do not conform to support the LGBT political message has continued against bakers, florists, and pizza shop owners. They essentially are using a political bludgeon to demand that America conform. The word in the *Humanist Manifesto* that rings in my ears when I read about these issues is *demand*. We demand! They most certainly do!

An aggressive demand that all people join humanist thinking is not in keeping with our theistic founding roots or our founding documents granting freedom of speech and thought.

It is likely a very small minority of the citizens who have same-sex attraction who have also chosen the path of the aggressive demand for approval. They have joined and have been spearheaded by aggressive humanists and Communists. The prescription of using a small number of people from a victim group mixed with a copious number of trained activists is the same mix that is present in any of the division that is created in our nation today. However, the difference with the LGBT movement is that it strikes at our spiritual roots and through the increased media attention, introduction of same-sex relationships into our daily entertainment, and utilizing public school to train pubescent children in homosexual behavior, that group has expanded.

In 2020, Walt Disney's organization, which traditionally spoke to the children of America, has a new movie coming out in the fall that will not only immerse children in homosexual acceptance but will also fill their hearts and minds with a transsexual character.

Next, the gay pride parades came in vogue and we saw on public display behaviors that ought to be private. Along with the display came a demand that pride for the behavior must be freely given. This coercion to embrace a lifestyle contrary to someone's deeply held religious beliefs is utterly absurd. It is absurd, unless you are a revolutionary who is using this means to accomplish the end of all traditional values. They continue to move us from a theist government, where people grant limited rights to governing authorities, to an atheist government, which holds all rights and authority and doles out small approved freedoms to some citizens while withholding them from others.

It is absurd to think that the public school system in California will begin to teach heroes in the classes by their sexual choices rather than their heroic deeds. Sexuality need never be addressed. It is personal and private. True service to mankind or personal accomplishment should be acknowledged. Why any group of individuals would want to diminish another's life of work and accomplishments to unseen private behavior cannot possibly be rational unless one sees it as another line of battle in this war against traditional theist values.

There are millions of Americans who have changed their shopping patterns and left Home Depot for Lowes, left Sears and Penney, as the corporations have become part of the pro-gay-pride aggression. I have noticed that the stock is down on both Penney and Sears. I believe many Americans feel much like I do. We do not have animosity against homosexual persons, no homophobia, no anger or hatred. We may have a bit of pity, a heartfelt compassion toward homosexuals. We have, however, a growing anger at the aggressive nature of a movement that demands special treatment and honor for something that should have neither given to it. No matter how many laws are passed or what aggressive hatred and dishonor is shown to our society by the gay activist group, organized by secular humanist revolutionaries, there will not be a change in the hearts and minds of people who feel that the attraction toward people of the same sex is foreign and opposes God's design. Ultimately, it is not something that most people want either to spend a great deal of time considering or to be demanded to approve of it or join in communal pride. We are, like the young man I spoke of earlier, a bit sick of the insistence.

The secular humanists have, as stated, co-opted this group of people because it suits their purpose in many ways. They have utilized the same methodology as seen in instituting atheism in public schools and institutions.

The method is to isolate a small minority of people that will serve the purpose of establishing the principles of secular humanism and drive traditional values out. The individual people are sheep being led along to perform the bidding of change agents. They are fed the lie that the culture hates homosexuals and are homophobic. They are convinced that anyone who is not for the homosexual agenda is their enemy. Overall, it is safe to assume they really are convinced that they are poor victims who need to band together to demand their rights. The truth is that they are not hated individually, but the homosexual poor fools in a battle where they are fighting an enemy that does not exist for an end they may really not even understand.

Because there are scriptures which address homosexual behavior as wrong, elite humanists at the top of their community-organizing game can use this as a wedge in theist churches. The Bible speaks of stealing, killing, gossiping, hating, dishonoring, adultery, as well as homosexuality. The area of homosexuality, however, speaks to the very design of God, as does the role of being a mother speak to the design of God. There are many areas where human beings fall short of God's perfect plan, but because this area can be used to drive a wedge in churches, weaken the core family, and serve to break down our cohesion as a people, the humanists have utilized it in their political and judicial war against traditions.

I have expressed purely personal views for a reason. They are how I feel. I am weary of being painted in broad strokes by silly, incompetent, incoherent news commentators with a brush of "intolerant bigot." I am a theist with no bigoted attitudes. But that does not mean that I do not have absolute values. It is wearisome for intolerant atheist revolutionaries to diminish me with foolish words that have no appropriate application. I believe many who read this feel as I do.

Those who wish to use the area of homosexuality as a great divider and as a means of wiping out greater and greater portions of our Christian heritage have been fortunate because, for the most part, people continue to dance all around the subject and never address it; meanwhile, the revolution of atheism, with all its ramifications, marches through our culture. Theists are unable to grasp what is going on. Listening to Conservative commentators, for me, is like watching a bunch of people standing in a 105-degree Tucson day—dancing all around a pool in their swimsuits but never jumping in! We never actually outline the revolution. We never identify the roots of the war and the ends that are close at hand. We just hover around, complaining that it is "hot."

Since we have failed to identify the plan that is being instituted, and where it is taking us, we are incapable of engaging in the war.

Well, hang in there, because one person's solution is forthcoming.

CHAPTER 7

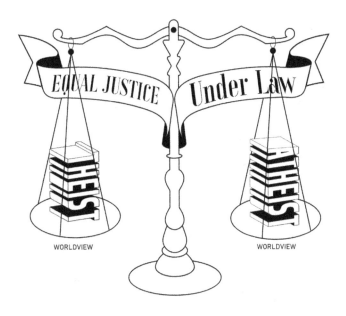

The Body of *Humanist Manifesto II*

The First Affirmation in *Humanist Manifesto II*

Religion

In the best sense religion may inspire dedication to the highest ethical ideals. The cultivation of moral devotion and creative imagination is an expression of genuine "spiritual" experience and aspiration.

We believe, however, that traditional dogmatic or authoritarian religions that place revelation, God, ritual or creed above human needs and experience do a disservice to the human species. Any account of nature should pass the tests of scientific evidence. In our judgment, the dogmas and myths of traditional religions do not do so. Even at this late date in history, certain elementary facts based upon the critical use of scientific reason have to be restated. We find insufficient evidence for belief in the existence of a supernatural; it is either meaningless or irrelevant to the question of the survival and fulfillment of the human race. As non-theists, we begin with humans not God, nature not deity. Nature may indeed be broader and deeper than we now know; any new discoveries however, will but enlarge our knowledge of the natural.

Some humanists believe we should reinterpret traditional religions and reinvest them with meanings appropriate to the current situation.

Such redefinitions, however, often perpetuate old dependencies and escapisms; they easily become obscurantist, impeding the free use of the intellect. We need, instead, radically new human purposes and goals.

We appreciate the need to preserve the best ethical teachings in the religious traditions of humankind, many of which we share in common. But we reject those features of traditional religious morality that deny humans a full appreciation of their own potentialities and responsibilities. Traditional religions often offer solace to humans, but as often, they inhibit humans from helping themselves or experiencing their full potentialities. Such institutions, creeds, and rituals often impede the will to serve others. Too often traditional faiths encourage dependence rather than independence, obedience rather than affirmation, fear rather than courage. More recently they have generated concerned social action, with many signs of relevance appearing in the wake of the "God is Dead.". But we can discover no divine purpose or providence for the human species. While there is much that we do not know, humans are responsible for what we are or will become. No deity will save us; we must save ourselves.

The introduction of *Humanist Manifesto II* outlines the reason for writing the document. This document was to:

1. clarify the previous document,

2. reassert humanist values, and

3. establish social intent or action for procuring the stated changes.

The assertion that "we must save ourselves" provides the fuel for this fire. Their agenda is placed in clear view for all to see. They will create a governmental structure that allows men to be in control and save the world.

The purpose remains to replace outdated, "dangerous" religious ideas and traditions with a new perspective for the twenty-first century. The revolution must lead the populace away from faith in a personal, prayer-hearing, prayer-answering God who provides salvation and a promise of eternal life. The revolution will create a dependence on one another. The new society must look from God and to itself and one another for solutions. The *plan* is to continue the revolution. As Goebbels said earlier, it must be complete—political, social, religious, academic, and economic.

The desire is to change and exchange the traditions, values, and thinking for the new system. While some suggest that they can "reinterpret traditional religions and reinvent them with meanings appropriate to the current situation," their stated goal is to fully replace the old with the new. All aspects of human life will exchange the Judeo-Christian beliefs, laws, traditions, and social norms with secular humanist dogma and fervor to social action and revolution.

This first statement of the second manifesto reiterates the humanist position and intentions. Having strengthened their initial plan, with this second document they make it clear that they will continue with great fervor to bring their worldview into every part of the social structure until the revolution is complete. They have enjoyed remarkable strides up to this time in the areas of law and education. They are about to make a full assault on removing God from all public matters and weaken the private faith of individual believers. The most important facet of the sexual revolution (LGBT movement) will complete the move away from the traditional families and religious structures that mirror our Founders'.

By the time of the writing of the second manifesto, the secular humanists had advanced their agenda by

1. reformulating educational policies, attitudes, and curriculum, from university through grade school

2. graduating several generations of teachers fully engaged in humanist thinking;

3. advancing the removal of God in the court, schools, and all public places; and

4. erasing an accurate account of our nation's history. The history taught today is replete both with additions of items that form the public conscience and with removals of both the heroes and principles which provide our nation its identity.

We have grouped our populations into isolated victim groups and now, in the midst of the coronavirus, have isolated people from one another and added masks to create an entirely impersonal isolation. The Blacks were to be our first victim group, then women, then gays, then Hispanics. The groups would cause continued division, which prepares the nation to fall to the power of the revolution. They are adamant to divide us as a people. The humanist motto could have been, "United they stand, divided we win." They desired for the American population to lose the unity we have always had. Their desire is for citizens to see themselves as a part of a fractured victim group. The greater this problem of division grows, the more urgent is the call for governmental intervention. The greater the governmental intervention, the more power would be granted to government and the less influence the individual would retain. I believe Dennis Prager says that "the individual citizen is shrinking".

Our Founders' governmental plan, where the citizen receives inalienable rights from God and grants limited, restricted powers to the government, is all but gone.

The number and scope of programs have grown as families deteriorate and victimization is capitalized on. The similarity of each government program is that at their heart they are humanists trying to make the world a better place by human effort alone. This is currently interpreted as the Progressive political thinking. It is fine to attach a name to the political direction; however, it does nothing to identify the foundational exchange that is taking place. We hear the term Progressive used to describe certain policies, but we have lacked the connection between it and the end society that is being structured. The end society is one without God and without national sovereignty. It is one where the government acts as God and a small group of elites will have absolute power and control over every resource. They will determine what will be handed out. Karl Marx's axiom will stand: "From each according to his ability, to each according to his need." The Progressive movement, which is the political arm of the Secular Humanist agenda, does not just intend to weaken the role of the individual citizen and strengthen the domination of government. In the end, the world citizen becomes the slave of the overlord, who determines your ability and your need. Because the Progressive political movement is the political arm of the humanist movement, it truly seeks to replace God in the lives of citizens with the government and those citizens who affirm Progressive political practices. The education system continues to turn out citizens with this point of view, and it starts all over again. This circuitous process, if fully and successfully implemented, should meet the goals stated in the first *Humanist Manifesto* of making the twenty-first century the humanist century. Where all the political structures, educational structures, laws, entertainment, and personally held beliefs will reflect a humanist mindset and, further, that humanism will fulfill the need for religious thought and actions.

We need to hearken back to the first manifesto for this statement:

> We are convinced that the time has passed for theism deism, modernism, and the several varieties of "new thought."

This second *Humanist Manifesto* was written in 1973. It restated the first principles set into place forty years earlier and expanded them. Edwin H. Wilson, a Unitarian pastor and one of the founders of the American Humanist Movement, and Paul Kurtz, best known as the Father of Secular Humanists, authored this document.

The quiet, critical steps for social transformation were in place, and their fruit was becoming evident. This second manifesto would build upon the first, acknowledging the broad social and legal changes that had already taken place. This manifesto would now prepare the social structure to move forward at a breathtaking pace. I wrote about my college experience earlier in order to establish the stage upon which these next sweeping changes in morals and religious attitudes would be played out upon.

Consider the Change in 1973

The *Humanist Manifesto II* was written in 1973.

Roe v. Wade was decided by the Supreme Court in 1973.

Federal funding of Planned Parenthood began in 1970. The initial funding was for birth control and family planning. By 1973, with the finding in the *Roe v. Wade* case, the federal government made massive increases to Planned Parenthood. These increases were to support their clinics and education. The focus of Planned Parenthood's attention was the same target as the humanists: the public schools. Sex education became a bedrock foundation for instructing children in a humanist worldview. The Planned Parenthood classroom instruction undermined parental religious instruction, as well as parental authority. It was designed to make the child (with the approval and support of their peers and school authorities) an autonomous segment of society, free to make their own personal decisions about their sexual activity. Children, while a member of a family under the parents' care and authority in every other aspect of their lives, were instructed that they were independent regarding their sexuality. When and with whom to engage in sexual activity was a purely personal decision each person must make for themselves. There was no moral training in the presentation of human sexuality, and it was never placed within the context of permanent marriage with the results of children.

The schoolchildren receiving this instruction would be required to have parental permission for the school nurse to administer a Tylenol for a headache, but in the specific area of sexuality, which establishes the bedrock of family and future, they were made autonomous. The consequences of random sexual activity are endless, but from a simplistic standpoint, they include physical disease, mental anguish, and pregnancy, resulting either in the life of a new child or an abortion, which terminates a life and may result in a lifetime of problems for both the father and mother of the child who was conceived. Nearly every state has had to face the legal question regarding the right for parents to be a part of the decisions made in the lives of their children in the area of contraception and abortion. The humanist-led pro-choice movement is adamantly opposed to the involvement of parents at any level. This position is consistent with the stated goals of the *Humanist Manifesto* and in keeping with their belief that the Judeo-Christian belief in God and eternity and judgment are all dangerous to human beings.

This was the first time in public school history where the federal government paid out huge amounts of money in the form of grants and contracts to a private business (Planned Parenthood) that, in turn, was granted access to the public school rooms of America where the greatest portion of our children spend nine months out of their year.

1. Planned Parenthood would be funded by the government with our tax dollars.

2. Planned Parenthood was given our classrooms, where they would establish their "business" (make no mistake with a revenue stream that exceeds one billion dollars per year—Planned Parenthood is a B-U-S-I-N-E-S-S), and a very successful one.

3. The business was set up in the classrooms of America, which is their target consumer. They would be able to hold a consumer audience captive to their teaching and products with no other competition.

If you are a businessman or a businesswoman, I imagine you would love those odds for your business success!

Planned Parenthood teaches their own brand of sex education with the weight of the approval of the public school system and federal government. This brand teaches children about sexual activity entirely apart from traditional moral values, and most certainly apart from the covenant and purpose of marriage. It teaches about sex without the assertion that there is a core family made up of a father, mother, and children. Thus was provided the retraining of children to achieve a new social structure in keeping with humanist values.

These sex education classes taught sexuality as a natural part of life and without the undesired end of procreation. In truth, our sexuality and the fruit of that act are the heart of any society. It is through procreation that family lines are established, and physical and mental heritages are passed from generation to generation. But unfortunately, the sex education classes did not have the purpose of teaching the grand plan for human sexuality, but merely the physical act of human sexuality and the means to avoid procreation.

The Planned Parenthood classes taught children about sexuality without instilling the values of the families, without teaching restraint. There was no admonition to curtail behavior patterns that would encourage sexual behavior apart from permanent commitment. The motto of Planned Parenthood sounds wonderful. Their stated goal was to "make every child a wanted child," or a planned parenthood. The instruction was that sex could begin with whomever one wished at any time in the person's personal maturity, but conceiving a child must be planned. An unplanned child should be terminated, and children engaging in sexual activity prior to wanting to be parents should learn to use contraceptives. If one has a mindset of zero population growth, contraception and abortion would not just be preferred but would be mandated to control the growth and stop the ticking population bomb.

This means of population control sounded logical and good to the humanistic mind, but it greatly missed the mark of the traditionalist that believes in a Creator God. Traditional parents who believed in conscientious courtship with parental oversight leading to a time of engagement and formal covenant commitment of marriage were outdated. These ideas deep in the heart of theists were set aside as the government foisted the humanist-agenda-funded programs that would separate parents from their children at increasingly earlier ages.

Christian family principles were considered outmoded, and the feminist movement was also put into the classroom, so the role of sexuality was no longer considered primarily from the aspect of family. We did not realize at that time that the social upheaval was being planned and directed to complete a revolution that would one day turn the populace into the slave of the state. The state would become God, and the elites the slave masters. The humanists, however, were aware that they were leading us to a humanist twenty-first century. The Christian heritage once held by the majority of citizens of our United States was to be ostracized from the classroom.

The introduction of sex education in the public schools, and the subsequent provision of contraceptive and abortion services in the public school system, brought about greater fundamental change in our social structure than any other since WWII.

The values about family and child-rearing, which had previously been taught and passed from generation to generation, were now in question. The nature and purpose of the family unit were being redefined and replaced. Up until this time, the family was pictured as the foundation of our social structure. It was the family that was to feed, clothe, and house and train children. Both parents were perceived as valuable and necessary to the process. America saw herself as imperfect but strong, consistent and industrious. We were full of invention, opportunity, and resilience and of individual character. We had an ideal before us even if we failed in some aspects. We knew what the family's job was and its relationship to the community and the nation and to the God of the Bible.

Can You Almost Hear the Rapid Drumroll, In Your Ear as the Change Sweeps Into Every Home, School, and Public Area?

The new generation of students (from kindergarten rooms to the university) would be taught that sexual activity was good and appropriate for anyone at any age with any other person, as long as both were willing and no unwanted child resulted. This was stunningly contrary to our former morality. The move to add gender and homosexual training to increasingly younger children will usher in the legal move that the Man Boy Love society and Ruth Bader Ginsburg have championed, which is to remove the "legal age of consensual sex," opening the door for children to be legally taken as sexual partners. While such an act may sound completely unthinkable today, I want you to consider how quickly we have traveled from a nation that believed we have two genders to today, where more than ninety are being identified by the LGBT community.

We must never remove the protection from children and allow them to become sexual fodder to the society. If you consider this unthinkable, consider this: We currently have teachers and doctors affirming the gender confusion of little children. Children as young as eight years old are being aided in their confusion with drugs, with idea of moving them into surgeries, which will change their lives forever. I personally consider this child abuse. We can see that there are those in the society that will do anything to advance the social breakdown. They will encourage a child that barely knows anything about life to make a decision they will live with every day of their lives. It seems to me, as a Christian traditionalist, that this is tantamount to child abuse, and the abusers should be arrested. However, it appears more nearly that the parent who attempts to protect a child he loves may become the one taken captive to the police state rather than the abuser.

This replacement of one social structure or social order for another was being coolly and deliberately completed. All the time traditionalists raised a cry of despair, they failed to understand the structure of humanism that was being implemented. They disagreed with the implementation, but they had no idea that what was being done in their schools was part of the social plan to rid the nation of a belief in the Judeo-Christian God of the Bible. They reacted to one battle front after another with no comprehensive understanding that the individual battles were a part of a well-designed war. This new humanist view of sex without restraint and the fulfillment of multiple sexual partners joined forces with the women's moment to hasten the breakdown of the traditional family structure and usher in the "village family", which we see today. Hillary Clinton's view of child rearing is that it is done by all the people in the community including the government. Government programs such as Head Start are to feed and instruct. Government afterschool programs are to house children for the time between school and parents coming home from work. Government food programs will feed the children. Government will provide homes and medical care. The "village" sends tax money to the elite government officials who in turn will send money back to government programs that are designed to train the children to be government units that are fully indoctrinated in the humanist worldview. In turn the children are loyal to the elites as they grow up and they will REMAIN obedient to the will of the state.

As classrooms throughout the country indoctrinated students, cute half-hour sitcoms designed for the young and the old inculcated the population with new cultural standards, which opposed biblical standards and principles. Young and old television characters entered our living rooms every week to approve of hooking up, living together. and divorce. The characters that held traditional values were included in the cast as fools, grumps, or judgmental. The lifestyle of the traditionalist was boring and colorless. Television reinforced this new thought. Movies, children's books, college texts, and popular novels all supported the same themes, and the social change was put into high gear.

The sex education classes grew in funding and time in the classroom. Sexually transmitted disease, unwanted pregnancy, and abortion were on the rise; these were all the wares of Planned Parenthood. The clinics provided birth control, exams, pregnancy tests, and of course, abortion. Some of those services came with a fee, but many were free to the client and paid for by the taxpayer.

In addition to Planned Parenthood, the federal and state government agencies were involved. They added funding to their county and city health-care programs, and all programs spoke from a humanist worldview.

How did young children (customers) know to go to the big business of Planned Parenthood? As mentioned earlier, they received both federal and local dollars and then were invited into the local classrooms to meet with their "customers." Students were, and are, taught a Planned Parenthood perspective on sex, parenting, and health.

Eventually, opt-out policies were passed by school boards to allow parents to opt their children out of the classes. My children were eventually among those who dutifully wrote essays in the library rather than remain through the classroom indoctrination. They were made to feel out of place. The students who remained in the classes were given materials by Planned Parenthood, and many school nurses would gladly accommodate the student's visit to or contact of Planned Parenthood for a student's reproductive needs. All this interaction was done without parental consent or knowledge. The confidentiality of this compartment of a child's life is consistent with the *Humanist Manifesto*. The child is autonomous from the parent and has a right to make their own decisions about right and wrong. Their ethical decisions are to be personal, situational, and managed without outmoded parental training. Children were, and are, being taught that they are the only ones who know if they are ready and the time is right for a sexual interaction.

The feminist movement was speeding ahead in conjunction with the indoctrination of the children. This assured the secular humanists that the assault on the family was putting pressure on the husband, the wife, and the children with equally momentous antitraditional training. While sex education and feminism were two different "battles," they were all part of the same war.

These were all structural social issues that were put into place. The schools, laws, churches, and entertainment were structures that both eliminated Christian principles and replaced them with humanist ideals.

The battle plan had been written, and the battles on the ground were raging. Liberated women explored their own sexual natures, teens had less supervision, and their role models were disappearing before their eyes. New government programs were started to respond to the movement of mothers leaving their homes to return to school and work. From the Head Start program (how could anyone not want a child to have a head start in life?) to after-school day-care programs, the role of the government expanded. The amount of collective tax dollars required to replace parenting, feeding, and housing children in all but the child's sleeping hours grew. The replacement of traditional family units was being implemented. Children were to be raised by state institutions, fed state-provided food, clothing, and education. The collective or village would raise the American children. The collective would inculcate them with values, and the entertainment community would serve to cement those values in their minds and hearts. The new child would grow up believing that the family is fluid, having different parents, brothers, sisters, aunts, uncles, and grandparents, depending on the day. They would grow up in a world that glamorized adultery, lying, and debauchery. They would believe that they were to live for today and that they could look to government to supply their needs. These values are all aligned with the humanist goal of replacing the traditional family with the government.

The facts are clear that Planned Parenthood has been used as one of many very effective tools in our public school system. Taxpayer-funded programs added approval and credibility to their message. The message has facilitated our social change. More to the point, Planned Parenthood is a vehicle used to facilitate many specific points in the *Humanist Manifesto I* and *II*.

Planned Parenthood Sex Education Classes teach:

1. There is no God to whom we are responsible, and children are autonomous from parents.

2. Mankind's decisions (including the decision to carry a child to full term) will determine our planetary outcome. Zero population growth is essential.

3. The body is a material biological mass, and we are to live to gain as much fulfillment of that body as possible. Just as the humanist motto was "doing good without God," their sexual

philosophy could be summed up as "having fun without consequence."

4. Nothing within the sexual realm is wrong, and conversely, nothing is more right than any other behavior.

5. Parenthood should be planned; other conception should be eliminated. Children can be cared for by any combination of human beings or one person equally well.

The humanist animosity and intolerance is not poured out equally on all religious belief systems. When the *Humanist Manifesto I* and *II* state that they must replace traditional values and beliefs, it is clear that they know that "traditional values and beliefs" refer specifically to Judeo-Christian values and beliefs. It was these Judeo-Christian beliefs that were reflected in our founding documents and the papers of our Founding Fathers. Our national artwork, its documents, and its business practices all looked to the Bible and Judeo-Christian values either emphatically or presumptively for their structure and order. The humanists are clear on who the enemy is. The widespread educational acceptance of Planned Parenthood's philosophy and presence in the nation's public school system enabled the revolutionary forces to move away from the nation of our Founders and toward the humanist twenty-first century.

As mentioned earlier, it is important here to consider that the humanists are not aggressive toward all religions. The California school system has instituted Muslim studies and Native American studies. In this case, students are encouraged to do studies that would include imagining that they are Islamic or Native American. They make their food, wear their dress, and study their commitments to their god. This type of religious practice is encouraged because these practices and belief structures support the strategy to move the nation away from its Judeo-Christian roots. It appears that any practice or tradition that has a hint of our Judeo-Christian roots is successfully shunned and actively outlawed.

The fact is that both the first and second *Humanist Manifesto* and their public actions are designed to eliminate the following religious tenets only:

1. A god who hears and answers prayer.

2. A god that provides salvation from sin.

3. A god who demands personal responsibility in this life, a promise of judgment, and then perhaps a life with him after death.

It is these religious beliefs that they consider "dangerous."

At the heart of the humanist message, there is no God to bow to but one's own desire. A humanist society must allow children to make their own choices. Experience is at the center of human fulfillment; hence, to curtail any person's full experience of any activity would contradict a humanist social structure.

That "experience is king" model of humanism is the parent to emotion-driven voting and emotion-driven life decisions. Emotion and experience reign in the heart of the American humanist. This is exactly contrary to the wise man or woman portrayed in the proverbs of the Bible.

The Second Affirmation in *Humanist Manifesto II*

Replace the Harmful Religion

Promises of immortal salvation or fear of eternal damnation are both illusory and harmful. They distract humans from present concerns, from self-actualization, and from rectifying social injustices. Modern science discredits such historic concepts as the "ghost in the machine" and the "separable soul" Rather, science affirms that the human species is an emergence from natural evolutionary forces. As far as we know, the total personality is a function of the biological organism transacting in a social and cultural context. There is no credible evidence that life survives the death of the body. We continue to exist in our progeny and in the way that our lives have influenced others in our culture.

Traditional religions are surely not the only obstacles to human progress. Other ideologies also impede human advance. Some forms of political doctrine, for instance, function religiously reflecting the worst features of orthodoxy and authoritarianism, especially when they sacrifice individuals on the alter of Utopian promise. Purely economic and political viewpoints, whether capitalist or communist, often function as religious and ideological dogma. Although humans undoubtedly need economic and political goals they also need creative values by which to live.

This second affirmation asserts that the religions that are the enemy to secular humanism are those who rest a belief in immortal salvation and eternal damnation. These religious beliefs are rooted in the Bible and are the named enemies. This enemy is also any value or tradition that permeates the culture and retains the flavor and lifestyle that would result from biblical training. It is upon this Bible that our Founders swore; it is the Bible that was placed in early public schools as a reading text. The Bible has been the text most widely referred to by wise men and women and our Founders. This Bible and the religious beliefs that spring from it are the enemies of the revolution; hence, the revolution must fully replace Christianity with an unbending, irreproachable, intolerant state religion of atheism. No vestige of Christianity will be allowed to remain.

This second affirmation is a restatement of the principle in the first *Humanist Manifesto* that the human being is born out of evolution and is only flesh. The public elimination of the soul and spirit from the human being literally changes everything. Our early writings, education, laws, public morals, and personal training have been established on the construct that we are many-faceted. A biblical construct would assume body, soul (mind, will, and emotion), and spirit. The humanist concept that we are flesh alone cannot take into account the damage that is done to the human soul at an early age when bombarded with continual sensuality and violence. It cannot take into account the poor character that will result from the soul steeped in the food, the entertainment, and gaming industries provide for our consumption.

This affirmation states that Capitalism is also an enemy of the humanist ideal. In truth, the removal of Capitalism is a crucial plank of the humanist revolutionary takeover. Capitalism grants the individual an ability to achieve and to prosper. It allows for competition, and while unprincipled men and women are able to gain from the system, it provides a way for principled, hardworking individuals to achieve vast goals and dreams. The elite will not be able to reign as sovereign over the masses as long as there are individuals able to prosper and apply personal energy and ingenuity to gain individual wealth. Humanism demands that Capitalism be destroyed.

The Third Affirmation in *Humanist Manifesto II*

Ethics

We affirm that moral values derive their source from human experience. Ethics is autonomous and situational, needing no theological or ideological sanction. Ethics stems from the human need and interest. To deny this distorts the whole basis of life. Human life has meaning because we create and develop our futures; Happiness and the creative realization of human needs and desires, individually and in shared enjoyment, are continuous themes of humanism. We strive for the good life, here and now. The goal is the pursue life's enrichment despite debasing forces of vulgarization, commercialization, bureaucratization, and dehumanization.

This is the revolutionary moral code that is outlined by the humanist doctrine as a replacement for the "outdated" Ten Commandments. Ethics are strictly personal and nontheological. Unlike the old moral values, which are being replaced, the new ethical standard is to be embraced by all without question or discussion. In the event someone questions these new moral standards, they will be silenced by the accusation of being judgmental, prudish, or phobic. The set of humanist ethical standards is not absolute like the Ten Commandments. They are fluid and situational. Stealing, murder, adultery, covetousness, and lying are each appropriate when done to serve a specific goal. There is no law that is absolute in the mind of the true humanist.

Our nation is a nation that was built upon the law, and the law is to be equally applied to every person; hence, whether one is a maid or the president, all must abide by the standard of law that is established. This equal treatment is entirely gone. The elite class, which is the political class who is moving the humanist revolution forward, has no moral law to which they must adhere. Anything that furthers the revolution is approved. The law is now used as a bludgeon to silence those who disagree with the elite talking points, not as a means to bring criminals to justice. Both public and private ethics are situational and autonomous. A close look at what was done to President Trump before his election and after his swearing in will attest to this truth.

I am writing this in 2021, having just completed a presidential election and still are held captive to this very sinister, deep, and thorough plot to stop Donald J. Trump. This attempt included CIA, FBI, Justice Department, heads of state, as well as foreign powers. The attempt was to curtail Donald Trump from becoming president in 2016 and, once they were unable to do that, to stop the effectiveness of his presidency and curtail his re-election. While we are told that investigations are ongoing, only history will tell what the outcome of this attempted coup will be. If all were still equal under the law, it is likely that a hundred people from the past president down to many of the highest-level government employees would be in prison for the balance of their lives.

We watch the law being thwarted and misused daily in regards to those involved in politics. If you are on the theist side of the political equation, you will be tarred and feathered. If you are on the humanist side, you will likely become the media's darling.

Whether or not to demand lawful behavior is now central to the debate in America. What was once considered a common social thread to all but the criminal class appears to have been severed. Lawful behavior is no longer asked of the elites. There is now one of the major political parties who is calling for either the abolition of the police or their defunding. Major cities are having crime waves, where murder is rising exponentially. We see on the nightly news a young gangster pouring paint and pushing an elderly woman on a walker who is trying to defend her property. There is seemingly no repercussion to the gang members. Buildings are being burned, cars burned, looting violence, and the demand for police to get on their knees and bow down to the gangs.

While one side of the law has turned a blind eye to evil behavior, the other side is equally concerning. The legal system may be used to strip a medical professional for caring for their patients, or put someone in jail and fine them harshly for using the incorrect pronoun when addressing someone. This is what we see as becoming the law in America today.

The tolerance for personal ethical standards applies to anyone within the revolution, but there is a complete intolerance for people who treasure and hold to traditional ethical standards that are absolute and find their roots in the Bible.

Since no one is required to answer to any authority but themselves, no person has the right to question any lifestyle. Since the child is autonomous from the parent, even the parent has no authoritative right to oppose a child's ethical standard.

Ten years ago most Americans would have said that it would be absurd and immoral to allow children to arbitrarily decide their gender day by day and use any bathrooms in the schools that they wish. Now it is the law in California. Although today children are still legally protected from adults who would sexually prey on them, I have suggested that within the next ten years we will see that wall of protection tumble and children will be fair game for anyone.

Based on their autonomous nature, children would be legally able to accept sexual relations with anyone of any age without the protection of parents or the legal system. This is the direction the current state religion is moving in our public schools. The religion of secular humanism is taught by word, deed, and practice. It is instilled in children through the choice of literature and the history that is taught. Make no mistake: the secular humanists believe that these values are simply taught and that there is no God who can speak to the heart or mind of an individual, which will overcome the persistent state training. They believe that the final vestiges of Judeo-Christian heritage are now in their hands.

The Fourth Affirmation in *Humanist Manifesto II*

Reason and Intelligence

Reason and intelligence are the most effective instruments that humankind possesses. There is no substitute: neither faith nor passion suffices in itself. The controlled use of scientific methods, which have transformed the natural and social sciences since the Renaissance, must be extended further in the solution of human problems. But reason must be tempered by humility, since no group has a monopoly of wisdom or virtue. Nor is there any guarantee that all problems can be solved or all questions answered. Yet critical intelligence, infused by a sense of human caring, is the best method humanity has for resolving problems. Reason should be balanced with compassion and empathy and the whole person fulfilled. Thus, we are not advocating the use of scientific intelligence independent of or in opposition to emotion, for we believe in the cultivation of feeling and love. As science pushes back the boundary of the known, man's sense of wonder is continually renewed and art, poetry, and music find their places, along with religion and ethics.

This principle of the manifesto is particularly mind-numbing for those who apply reason along with information to arrive at a conclusion. The inconsistent, seemingly irrational nature of the legal system and governmental practices are the cause of the deepest frustrations for American citizens who adhere to the Founders' principles. They serve to create a quiet, helpless desperation in the soul of thoughtful citizens.

Some of the frustrating inconsistencies have already been noted, but to clarify, let me mention just a few more.

We are a nation in deep debt. Joblessness plagues our families, yet when given an opportunity to install a pipeline from Canada, our neighboring nation, through the states to bring oil into the country at a more reasonable rate, it is declined. This pipeline would add high-paying jobs. It would provide a national boon to the economy, not only in jobs, but also in the monthly costs of the average American family who uses petroleum for their cars, homes, and countless other things. It would positively affect our food prices both in the cost of farming and the cost of moving goods to market. It would positively affect our federal and state budgets, but most dramatically our defense budget. The cost of fuel to power state and federal vehicles and, most notably, our armed services would be affected. It would do wonders toward relieving our national debt, and there have been no indications that it is environmentally unfriendly. This pipeline appears to pass the "reason and intelligence" threshold, unless you are a humanist revolutionary, and then the answer would be no! The pipeline would enhance Capitalism, and Capitalism is an enemy of the humanist system. The pipeline would help protect our national sovereignty by strengthening our failing system. The humanist ideal is to destroy our sovereignty in order to move the United States into the "planetary" system. While the pipeline meets the standard of "reason and intelligence," it ultimately supports our traditional Capitalist system and hence is the enemy of the humanists.

Let's consider another example.

A law is passed in a state to provide a service the federal government is charged with but fails to do in the area of illegal immigration. The federal government immediately sues the state, which costs millions of dollars and weakens the state's ability to protect its citizens and its finances. This is outside the realm of "reason and intelligence" if you are a traditional thinker who believes in our Founders' principles of states right and national sovereignty. If you are a revolutionary, however, it meets the tests of wasting the citizen's money, frustrating the citizen's rights to protect their property, and imposing a certain powerlessness over the individual citizen. This scenario occurred in Arizona during the Obama administration. The state was being overrun with illegal aliens, and we gave the authority for our sheriff to request to see proof of citizenship in the event someone was stopped for some other reason. This was a reasonable state law to protect citizens; however, in this case the feds used its power and the citizens' money to sue the state. The state wanted to have the laws concerning illegal aliens kept. The federal government did not wish to keep them. This picture of no concern either for law or the protection of our sovereignty will be the norm of the future. This will be the way of the final revolution, where a small number of elites will have ultimate power over the citizens in the United States and its laws. The citizens will be helpless to stop the forward motion of the steamroller that is about to come upon them.

Here is another real-life example.

An old well-loved guitar company purchases wood that meets all the export standards of the country it is purchased from. Once the wood is in their warehouses as material ready to use, the EPA sets a lawsuit against them regarding their use of a species of wood. This would fail the "reason and intelligence" standard when considered on the surface, unless one understands that the revolutionary goal is to stop Capitalism and to eliminate all opposition to the forward momentum of the humanist planetary system. When it is considered in this light, it is easy to see that it is fully reasonable to the revolutionaries. This served to quiet a company whose political opinion opposed the current humanist sweep. The lawsuits tied up company resources and shrunk their company wealth and strength. The attempt to destroy one small piece of the Capitalist puzzle would have the additional value of sending a message to all other companies that would dare to cross the controlling elite's rules over law and common business practices. If this sounds like the Mafia, it is not—it is far worse. Everyone will bow under the heavy hand of the intolerant humanist machine.

One more instance.

The Boeing company decides to build a plant in Arkansas where they will not fall under the debilitating demands of the union that is curtailing their company growth, stability, and success.

The government has suits filed against them for so doing. This does not meet the "reason and intelligence" rule, unless one considers once again that this government assault against individual business is a method of gaining the much-desired national control over anyone who still has financial power.

It represents a movement away from traditional Capitalism in our corporate world, which grants the forward motion toward the humanist one-world economic system.

This use of the court system against businesses and states have also been used to eliminate Judeo-Christian traditions in our public school system and institute atheism as the state religion and provides the forward momentum toward a one-world theological system.

We could fill the pages of a book with instances of an entire lack of the exercise of reason in all areas that concern the implementation of the revolution. In the cases noted above, the assault is against states' rights and the rights of citizens to engage in profitable business practices. The bully has been the federal government, which is exercising increasing powers over every aspect of business and life in order to move the humanist ideal forward.

Illegal immigration fits secular humanists on several levels; it promotes breaking down of national sovereignty and weakens the United States as the voting population will be infused with people who do not have any understanding of our core values. This voting population may ensure the forward movement of the demise of the United States, giving rise to the one-world government and the redistribution of goods and services through the hands of the elites who will control this government.

These situations illustrate the exercise of absolute power of the federal government against the best interests of the populace, against the best interests of companies that earn money and drive jobs, and against individual states. None of these outcomes make sense to the common mind, but since they promote the *Humanist Manifesto* agenda, they are in perfect harmony, with reason in the mind of the revolutionaries.

The Fifth Affirmation in *Humanist Manifesto II*

The Individual

> The preciousness and dignity of the individual person is a central humanist value. Individuals should be encouraged to realize their own creative talents and desires. We reject all religious, ideological, or moral codes that denigrate the individual, suppress freedom, dull intellect dehumanize personality. We believe in maximum individual autonomy consonant with social responsibility. Although science can account for the causes of behavior, the possibilities of individual freedom of choice exists in human life and should be increased.

This principle appears to grant complete freedom to the individual. It appears that the secular humanist would supply political action, which would enhance the ability for the individual to succeed in business ventures and to have a system of taxation that would allow one to climb any ladder or reach any star. It appears that the individual would be free to worship openly with a grateful heart in any setting and be free to set their children to work at their own passions to succeed and flourish. This appears to be a promise of autonomy and appears to assume freedom *from* government restraint. The freedom promised by this affirmation in the manifesto has nothing to do with the autonomy that we just considered.

The freedoms here are twofold.

First, the first word that indicates their idea of freedom is the catchphrase "Dignity of the individual person." The traditional use of the word *dignity* would picture a stalwart gentleman or gentlewoman firmly fixed in unshakable moral values which represent their faith in God and recognition of their accountability to Him. The secular humanist usage of human dignity must be understood within the context of their entire document as well as their legislative agenda, and support of social engineering groups.

The secular humanist use of individual dignity is in the context of the right to live or the right to extinguish your own life—i.e., the right to die, or commonly known as assisted suicide. This includes the right to have a doctor or others terminate your life at your own will and, of course, the right to be a doctor to terminate the lives of those who request it. This human dignity is more directly addressed in a later affirmation.

Second, the second statement of "Autonomy consonant with social responsibility" enjoins our individual freedom to society's best interest—no freedom at all! We can individually be encouraged to realize our individual talents and desires *if* it has no negative impact upon the environment (as gauged by them) and *if* it has no negative impact on the economic structure (as gauged by them). Consider for a moment this secular humanist movement engaging in a thought process surrounding a business or corporation who is wildly successful by any free market standard. They provide a product people want at a price they are willing to pay. Via this market model, millions of families are supported, both through direct employment of people as well as the employment of the suppliers of goods and materials to their business. Now, suppose that the head of this corporation has the temerity to express their own personal views, which are contrary to the secular humanist revolution and support the traditional documents and values of the United States. The secular humanist media machine will move into high gear to destroy the corporation, the individual, and to further attempt to bring as much shame and silence as the population will allow. Think Hobby Lobby.

There is no freedom and no autonomy in the secular humanist state. There are only the intolerant parameters that the state establishes and are instituted for the corporate good to ensure that the twenty-first century is the humanist century. One need only consider the Twitter, YouTube, Facebook and Parler blackout imposed upon millions of citizens who expressed belief in 2020 voter fraud. The blackout occurred right before the inauguration in 2021 in order to curtail any public discourse outside of the discourse "allowed." The First Amendment was eliminated by the power of the elitist few.

The one area that may presuppose personal autonomy is in sexuality. Any type of sexual involvement is appropriate and encouraged, save monogamous lifetime marriage commitments. Fifteen years ago, we could scarcely have believed that so many of our citizens would consider same-sex marriage a viable option. Today, the people under thirty fail to see its effects on the very foundation of the family. Redefining marriage supports the redefinition of the family. This is the autonomous behavior that is alluded to in this fifth affirmation.

This system of moral autonomy is extended only to those who do not embrace a prayer-hearing God, whom they look to for eternal life and salvation from sin. Anyone with the aforementioned traditional moral construct is dangerous and must be silenced at all costs. The secular humanist moral autonomy entirely rejects any absolute moral authority.

Absolute and punitive authority will rest with the state and will be brought to bear against any individual or company which attempts to design their own business with financial success as a primary goal. This authority comes to bear against an individual who desires freedom to use their land in a way that is beneficial for them. It may be used against an individual in choosing how to build a home that suits their personal needs. It may be exercised against a family who chooses to educate their children outside the state system. It now comes to bear against individuals who desire to have a family farm. This autonomous power will also be exercised against citizens based on their political beliefs. Since the children are autonomous from parents in the humanist structure, it follows that under this affirmation the state will have a right to step in and exercise its absolute power to protect children from their parents' outdated religious and moral codes, which contradict the *Humanist Manifesto*. These practical areas of life are soon to be subject by law to the goals of the revolutionaries.

The Sixth Affirmation in *Humanist Manifesto II*

Sexuality

In the area of sexuality, we believe that intolerant attitudes, often cultivated by orthodox religions and puritanical cultures, unduly repress sexual conduct. The right to birth control, abortion and divorces should be recognized. While we do not approve of exploitive, denigrating forms of sexual expression, neither do we wish to prohibit, by law or social sanction, sexual behavior between consenting adults. The many varieties of sexual exploration should not in themselves be considered "evil." Without countenancing mindless permissiveness or unbridled promiscuity (copied as written). A civilized society should be a tolerant one. Short of harming others or compelling them to do likewise, individuals should be permitted to express their sexual proclivities and pursue their lifestyles as they desire. We wish to cultivate the development of a responsible attitude toward sexuality, in which humans are not exploited as sexual objects in which intimacy, sensitivity and respect and honesty in interpersonal relations are encouraged. More education for children and adults in an important way of developing awareness and sexual maturity.

The heart of this sixth principle goes far beyond the encouragement of consensual sexual activity between adults. It bludgeons the traditionalist with the well-worn accusation of "intolerance." May we consider that the intolerance is, in fact, on the humanist side of this battle. There is an intolerance for the teaching of traditional sexual moral values in the public education setting. I believe there is a time coming very soon when even to teach or discuss the biblical purpose and the biblical model for human sexuality in the privacy of home or churches will be constrained. Thus is the power of the intolerant state religion. Thus is the animosity of secular humanists toward traditional thinkers. This state religion will allow freedom to only one group, secular humanists. Traditional believers, along with their beliefs, will be trampled underfoot.

The true humanist abhors the idea of connecting sexuality as the means to procreation and child-rearing. They want human sexuality to be couched in terms of personal fulfillment, as a sport, apart from its creative purpose. They are working tirelessly to redefine the family. Remember the play brought to my granddaughter's school? One of the main themes was the redefinition of the family unit. Genetic roots are abhorrent to the true secular humanist. All people are biological material; heritage is of little to no value to them.

The plan states here that "more education is necessary" for children and adults in important ways of developing awareness of sexual maturity. Make no mistake—the plan is taking us down the road to childhood autonomy so that children of any age can be engaged in the sexual arena. The humanist desire is to break down any inhibition for sexual activity and to have sexuality independent from family. This would ultimately take children out from under their parents' protection, and it may most likely deny parents the right to train their children in the moral values that reflect their family's religious values. It frees children to explore their own desire for sexual fulfillment as they are led by educators and adults with a secular humanist agenda. It further expresses that the children more nearly "belong" to the state than to their parents.

To a theist with a traditional worldview of the threefold person of body, soul, and spirit, it would deny parents the right to train the soul (mind, will, and emotion) of the child to control their body and to direct their actions out of the power and presence of God's Spirit dwelling in them. Children would have their sexuality stirred up so early in life that their spirit and soul would be quieted under the power of their physical drives. This pictures a perfect world for the secular humanist. The introduction of sexual ideas to a young child also serves as "grooming" the child for pedophilia. The biblical picture of man and woman joined in the sexual union portrays two becoming one. The mind, soul, and spirit completely intertwined with another person to, in some mysterious way, complete each other. The hookup mentality pictures an empty, soulless existence to one who embraces Judeo-Christian theistic values, yet it will be the existence that the humanist elites will insist on providing in the schools as an instruction in family life.

Consider the use of five-year-old children being introduced to homosexuality as a way of life in the "safe" environment of a classroom by their teacher, who represents their trusted mommy or daddy figure. Consider that they are introduced to those homosexual people as heroes to admire. Consider that these teachers have control over the children and the children are given autonomy from their parents. Consider that laws can be put into place to forbid parents from contradicting the teaching of homosexual practice that the school is providing. This may sound like a faraway scenario, but this is the essence of a program that is now part of the California State school system this year. This affirmation sets the stage for the legal action against a traditional Judeo-Christian parent and their instruction to their children. Can you begin to see that this is an action plan drawn up for the revolution in America? Our failure to address all these issues as one specific revolution leaves traditionalists helpless to address the takeover. The program that has begun in California could not have been done fifteen years ago; this has been a process that is unfolding. This revolution had to be done one step at a time, where one worldview was systematically being charged as intolerant and removed, while another system, dubbed as tolerant, was being instituted. In fact, it is the humanist system that is entirely intolerant.

The Seventh Affirmation in *Humanist Manifesto II*

Democratic Society

To enhance freedom and dignity the individual must experience a full range of civil liberties in all societies. This includes freedom of association, and artistic scientific, and cultural freedom. It also includes a recognition of an individual's right to die with dignity, euthanasia, and the right to suicide. We oppose the increasing invasion of privacy, by whatever means, in both totalitarian and democratic societies. We would safeguard, extend, and implement the principles of human freedom evolved from the Magna Carta to the bill of Rights, the Rights of Man and the Universal Declaration of Human Rights.

The right to take one's life when one desires to do so is the ultimate humanistic act. If we affirm there is no God and no accounting for our individual actions on this earth, one may freely decide when to end their life. The moment of death for the traditional theist belongs to God. For man to usurp God's hand in this decision is the ultimate expression of a faith that there is no God and there is no further existence.

When parsing the words in this seventh affirmation and examining them in light of the context of the entire plan, one easily understands that the enhanced freedom and dignity of the individual do not and will not include freedoms of artistic, associative, and cultural nature. Such freedoms inspire individual love of God, fealty for traditional spiritual dogma and truths, and worship of God within the context of art and culture.

These cultural expressions that show love and worship of a prayer-hearing God will be locked behind closed doors and hushed within the minds of the citizen, who senses the price to be paid if their heartfelt personal belief leaves their lips!

The list of documents in this affirmation oddly states that the human freedoms evolved *from* the Magna Carta to the Bill of Rights and finally ended up in the fully evolved document of the Universal Declaration of Human Rights (a secular humanist document). For the sake of those who may have forgotten the Magna Carta, I reprint the very beginning of that document here:

> KNOW THAT BEFORE GOD, for the health of our soul and those of our ancestors and heirs, to the honor of God, the exaltation of the holy Church, and the better ordering of our kingdom, at the advice of our reverend fathers Stephen, archbishop of Canterbury, primate of all England, and cardinal of the holy Roman Church, Henry archbishop of Dublin, William bishop of London, Peter bishop of Winchester, Jocelin bishop of Bath and Glastonbury, Hugh bishop of Lincoln, Walter Bishop of Worcester, William bishop of Coventry, Benedict bishop of Rochester, Master Pandulf subdeacon and member of the papal household, Brother Aymeric master of the knighthood of the Temple in England, William Marshal earl of Pembroke, William earl of Salisbury, William earl of Warren, William earl of Arundel, Alan de Galloway constable of Scotland, Warin Fitz Gerald, Peter Fitz Herbert, Hubert de Burgh seneschal of Poitou, Hugh de Neville, Matthew Fitz Herbert, Thomas Basset, Alan Basset, Philip Daubeny, Robert de Roppeley, John Marshal, John Fitz Hugh, and other loyal subjects:
>
> (1) FIRST, THAT WE HAVE GRANTED TO GOD, and by this present charter have confirmed for us and our heirs in perpetuity, that the English Church shall be free, and shall have its rights undiminished, and its liberties unimpaired. That we wish this so to be observed, appears from the fact that of our own free will, before the outbreak of the present dispute between us and our barons, we granted and confirmed by charter the freedom of the Church's elections—a right reckoned to be of the

greatest necessity and importance to it—and caused this to be confirmed by Pope Innocent III. This freedom we shall observe ourselves, and desire to be observed in good faith by our heirs in perpetuity.

Now, printed below is the *document* that the humanists believe we have evolved to: the preamble and first declaration of the Universal Declaration of Human Rights adopted by the United Nations:

Preamble

Whereas recognition of the inherent dignity and of the equal and inalienable rights of all members of the human family is the foundation of freedom, justice and peace in the world,

Whereas disregard and contempt for human rights have resulted in barbarous acts which have outraged the conscience of mankind, and the advent of a world in which human beings shall enjoy freedom of speech and belief and freedom from fear and want has been proclaimed as the highest aspiration of the common people,

Whereas it is essential, if man is not to be compelled to have recourse, as a last resort, to rebellion against tyranny and oppression, that human rights should be protected by the rule of law,

Whereas it is essential to promote the development of friendly relations between nations,

Whereas the peoples of the United Nations have in the Charter reaffirmed their faith in fundamental human rights, in the dignity and worth of the human person and in the equal rights of men and women and have determined to promote social progress and better standards of life in larger freedom,

Whereas Member States have pledged themselves to achieve, in co-operation with the United Nations, the promotion of universal respect for and observance of human rights and fundamental freedoms,

Whereas a common understanding of these rights and freedoms is of the greatest importance for the full realization of this pledge,

Now, Therefore THE GENERAL ASSEMBLY proclaims THIS UNIVERSAL DECLARATION OF HUMAN RIGHTS as a common standard of achievement for all peoples and all nations, to the end that every individual and every organ of society, keeping this Declaration constantly in mind, shall strive by teaching and education to promote respect for these rights and freedoms and by progressive measures, national and international, to secure their universal and effective recognition and observance, both among the peoples of Member States themselves and among the peoples of territories under their jurisdiction.

Article 1.

All human beings are born free and equal in dignity and rights. They are endowed with reason and conscience and should act towards one another in a spirit of brotherhood.

Note, if you will, the absence of any mention of God and the replacement of the words *dignity, rights, reason,* and *brotherhood.* These terms are the vocabulary of the secular humanists. The "rights" of the individual and the good of the whole are two terms found repeated. They are typical to be found as a purpose for suing individuals, companies, etc. in order to reorder our law to reflect no absolutes.

By hearkening back to the Magna Carta and including the United

Nations Universal Declaration of Human Rights, one easily sees that the secular humanists are laying a foundation for a one-world governing body. The language is strictly humanist and would provide a Progressive political agenda.

This language asserts the individual right to die, and in a world of shortages, it will also eventually grant the power to a body of individuals to select who will live.

Public schools regularly have students do a "lifeboat exercise," as before mentioned in this book, which gives students the experience in assessing individual value to the collective in order to determine who they will choose to live and who they will choose to die. They decide who will use resources and who will be cast out of the boat. This affirmation lays the groundwork for what will be the legal battles that will set the legal framework for social decisions regarding how to allocate scarce resources.

The Eighth Affirmation in *Humanist Manifesto II*

Democracy—the Vocabulary of Redistribution

We are committed to an open and democratic society. We must extend participatory democracy in its true sense to the economy, the school, the family, the workplace and voluntary associations. Decision-making must be decentralized to include widespread involvement of people at all levels—social, political and economic. All persons should have a voice in developing the values and goals that determine their lives. Institutions should be responsive to expressed desires and needs. The conditions of work education, devotion and play should be humanized. Alienating forces should be modified or eradicated and bureaucratic structures should be held to a minimum. People are more important than Decalogue's, rules, prescriptions or regulations.

This affirmation is actively being implemented every single day. The terms appear generous and inclusive, but in fact, it complements the other directives in both documents and works to break down the family and moral fiber, as well as Judeo-Christian beliefs and traditions. Let's explore it closely and see if we can view it in light of the *revolutionary* change being called for.

The secular humanists are dedicated to a democratic society (mob rule), not a representative form of government, or a republic, such as we have been given. The republic we have is expressed by the rule of law within the Constitution. The participatory democracy they envision in the school, family, workplace, and voluntary associations will be expressly humanized (i.e., made atheistic in nature, stripped of every vestige of Christian thought, belief, expression, and tradition). The "all persons" who should have a voice in developing values and goals that determine their lives would include all persons who do not have expressed belief in a prayer-hearing, salvation-providing God. Unwavering and absolute values have no place in the system that is described. Ultimately, they will want to do away with our electoral college which allows people from unpopulated states to have an influence in electing a president.

Note that any alienating forces should be modified or eradicated— that would be the code language for Bernard Shaw's solution to the Jews of World War II. This solution of modification or eradication would be applied to all people of faith unwilling to commit themselves to the new design of the secular humanist society.

The Ninth Affirmation in *Humanist Manifesto II*

Separation of Church and State

The separation of church and state and separation of ideology and state are imperatives. The state should encourage maximum freedom for different moral, political, religious, and social values in society. It should not favor any particular religious bodies through use of public monies nor espouse a single ideology and function thereby as an instrument of propaganda or oppression, particularly against dissenters.

Taken as a single statement, this seems like a highly "reasonable" goal but is, in fact, insidious in nature. The separation of church and state has been the single most successful argument utilized in the United States courtrooms to replace various theist traditions with an intolerant atheist social construct. It has been used to remove traditional moral beliefs, artwork, commonly held theist rules, such as the Ten Commandments, and to usher in the intolerant religion of atheism as our state religion. While it appears that we are not "favoring" any particular religious bodies, through the use of public monies, in fact, we have become rigorously fiscally supportive of a religious revolution in our nation. We are demanded to embrace atheism, with the secular humanists' documents as our guide.

We need a contrast to the demand for the separation of church and state, which is faithfully used by the secular humanist as a means of instituting atheism as the state religion with the language of our First Amendment.

Congress shall make no law respecting an establishment of religion or prohibiting the free exercise thereof.

The beliefs of our Founding Fathers, as expressed in the First Amendment, guaranteed freedom of religion. Their intent was well-documented in their private letters and speeches. Their actions also spoke volumes about their intent. Prayer prior to public deliberations was common practice, and public monies were used for the publication of Bibles. I refer you to the WallBuilders, many books written by David Barton, to verify this statement. All written forms of communication, from the Mayflower Compact to the Declaration of Independence, as well as the Constitution itself reflect the Founders' firm belief in God, and specifically the God of the Bible, who is personal, prayer-hearing, and-salvation providing. Most reveal a devotion to Jesus Christ. They had a continuous and deep dependency on this prayer and God. All must agree that it would not have been the Founders' intent to separate religion from the public life but rather not to allow the government to dictate a single religion or establish a single state religion.

In fact, the "separation of church and state" legal argument in the hands of decidedly cunning ACLU legal teams, and argued before decidedly humanist judges, has formed a body of precedent law that, should we hope to stop the forward motion and reverse this revolution, will take much time, effort, and money to accomplish. It will require many legal battles at the hands of skilled lawyers. The work to return rights and freedom to citizens holding Judeo-Christian thought in modern-day America will be equal to the battle that began this great nation. The first step in attempting to salvage our nation and reinstate religious freedom in America is to acknowledge what has happened and who is in charge.

In summary, the ninth declaration was to remove both theist religious thought and history from public education and the public forum in the United States. It would be replaced with the single intolerant religion of atheism, in the form of secular humanism, utilizing these documents as the **blueprint for the new world order**. In the guise of having an absence of religion and therefore no preference *for* a religion, atheism has been established as the state religion! It is crucial to wade through the two documents carefully in order to ascertain the degree that this religion has already been established and is being taught as the *exclusive* religion in our public school system.

The Tenth Affirmation in *Humanist Manifesto II*

Economy

Humane societies should evaluate economic systems not by rhetoric or ideology, but by whether or not they increase economic well-being for all individuals and groups, minimize poverty and hardship, increase the sum of human satisfaction, and enhance the quality of life. Hence the door is open to alternative economic systems.

We need to democratize the economy and judge it by its responsiveness to human needs, testing results in terms of the common good.

This is a crucial part of the humanist goals and is being aggressively implemented on several levels. Media and educators treat citizens with a "victim" mentality. They demand that government provide food, clothing, health care, minimum livable wage, childcare, and education (through advanced degrees) has been fast-tracked via the COVID-19 pandemic. We find these demands for all the citizens of the world in *Humanist Manifesto 2000*. In the fully implemented world government, the elites will have the right to take from those who have more than their basic needs. *This is redistribution*. What our citizens do not realize is that one day even the most basic provision to American citizens may seem like a king's ransom to citizens in other nations of the world. When a worldwide redistribution takes place, the citizens that are economically the lowest of the low in the United States will be painfully required to give up that which they believe they own into the hands of the elite controlling unit. They will then receive back the share of the world resources the governing authorities deem fit. This redistribution on a planetary scale is the endgame of the secular humanist worldwide plan. Make no mistake: the elite few who will do the distribution will be drunk with extravagant living and power beyond our wildest imaginations. The ruling class will have unearned abundance beyond measure. The slave class will have whatever the ruling class decides is necessary.

Let's break it down:

1. Overthrow the free enterprise economic system.

2. Take the responsibility from the individual to work, save, and increase their own economic well-being.

3. Give the responsibility of social justice and redistribution to the government.

4. The new government would be economically responsive to

human need. It would provide good results to the common good. No longer would the individual work to provide for their personal desire. The government would determine what was good for the collective and be the final arbiter of all goods and economic services and personal wealth.

Traditional Americans thought from the perspective of the free enterprise system teaches that personal need and want is the fire that spurs an individual's personal productivity and inventive genius. This new system is choreographed, if you will, from an ever-present elite who knows what is best for all. This methodology will serve to discourage the basic American work ethic of individual effort, hard work, and thrifty behavior. Our current system of free enterprise is one where success is born out of stable and supportive family and community relationships, a good reputation, and competitive skills. In our current free enterprise economic system, the government's job is to get out of the way of people and markets. Do not overregulate, and do not control unnecessarily; allow the people's demand for products to fuel the creativity of entrepreneurs and businesses to supply those goods and services. This free enterprise allows a person's training and abilities to make way for his services. It balances wages with the supply of those services available and the quality of the service given.

This free market economy is anathema to the system the "we" the tenth affirmation above describes. The "we" in this directive is a small group of elites who want to control the world. They are revolutionaries who hope to institute a worldwide economic system where they will control and redistribute the wealth of the world. This fact is made crystal clear in *Humanist Manifesto 2000*.

The Eleventh Affirmation in *Humanist Manifesto II*

Equality

The principle of moral equality must be furthered through elimination of all discrimination based upon race, religion, sex, age or national origin. This means equality of opportunity and recognition of talent and merit. Individuals should be encouraged to contribute to their own betterment. If unable, then society should provide means to satisfy their basic economic, health and cultural needs, including wherever resources make possible, a minimum guaranteed annual income. We are concerned for the welfare of the aged, the infirm, the disadvantaged, and also for the outcasts—mentally retarded, abandoned or abused children, the handicapped, prisoners, and addicts—for all who are neglected or ignored by society. Practicing humanists should make it their vocation to humanize personal relations.

We believe in the right to universal education. Everyone has a right to the cultural opportunity to fulfill his or her unique capacities and talents. The schools should foster satisfying and productive living. They should be open at all levels to any and all: the achievement of excellence should be encouraged. Innovative and experimental forms of education are to be welcomed. The energy and idealism of the young deserve to be appreciated and channeled to constructive purposes.

We deplore racial religious, ethnic, or class antagonisms. Although we believe in cultural diversity and encourage racial and ethnic pride we reject separations which promote alienation and set people groups against each other; we envision an integrated community where people have maximum opportunity for free and voluntary association rights for both women and men to fulfill their unique careers and potentialities as they see fit, free of invidious discriminations.

The "dramatic drumroll of revolution" should again be beating in our ears as we read and comprehend what this revolutionary statement will look like in the institution of legislation, programs, government subsidies, unrest in the streets, and at last, the undermining of our entire Constitution and way of life.

When this eleventh declaration is fully implemented, it will be the end of our free enterprise economic system, the end of the great experiment called America. It will be the fully enforced system of Socialism and redistribution of wealth.

This affirmation assures the completion of a new social order. It is *not* that our traditional system contradicts many of the stated goals in the affirmation. Our nation has, from its early days, supported education. We already deplore racial, religious, ethnic, and class antagonisms. This new society goes further to *demand* specific behaviors and attitudes from the individual citizen. It envisions a citizen formulated to fit into their pattern. Further, this society creates a citizen whose expectations rest in government control and largesse. The citizen who has been given the "rights" to certain services or life outcomes from its government may look to that entity to provide those ends. Once again, this affirmation pictures a government that will determine a minimum annual income, and then they will strip the wealth from anyone who lives above that base level to redistribute their wealth to others. They will control "collective" funds to ensure diversity and educational opportunities even if there is no job available at the end of the educational process.

There is a funny twist in this new social order. They will deplore anything that causes separation and division—except their intolerant religious system. The only group left that could cause a flurry of contention would be the Christian community, who may still remain staunch in their desire for open worship of the one true prayer-hearing God, who, as Creator, has power over both the giving and taking of life. These Christians may still abhor abortion and may teach their children the principles of godly marriage and child-rearing. They will hold to open prayer and thanksgiving to God and desire to share their faith with those who care to hear it. They will teach their children the biblical purpose for sexuality and expect their children to embrace it. They will, in all things, oppose the atheist worldview the secular humanists demand of them. While this affirmation states that they deplore religious antagonisms, they will, in fact, deplore the traditional Judeo-Christians and seek to silence or be rid of them.

What Americans (who now seem to embrace the revolution and look increasingly to government for their daily bread) fail to grasp is that when the redistribution really gets underway, even the most poverty-stricken American who lives at a level of luxury compared to much of the rest of the world will have their luxury redistributed and their basic lifestyle redefined by the absolute power of the governing authority. In the end, the populations of the world will be kept at a minimum-and-equal lifestyle, their reproduction controlled, their ability to produce and succeed controlled—everything will ostensibly be fair, but nothing, in the end, will enhance freedom or creativity. Nothing will provide true freedom of religion, worship, industry, or association. Those will all be dictated by the elite, who will control the masses.

The Twelvth Affirmation in *Humanist Manifesto II*

World Community

We deplore the division of humankind on nationalistic grounds. We have reached a turning point in human history where the best option is to transcend the limits of national sovereignty and to move toward the building of a world community in which all sectors of the human family can participate. Thus, we look to the development of a system of world law and a world order based upon transnational federal government. This would appreciate cultural pluralism and diversity. It would not exclude pride in national origins and accomplishments nor the handling of regional problems on a regional basis. Human progress however can no longer be achieved by focusing on one section of the world. Western or Easter, developed or underdeveloped. For the first time in human history, no part of humankind can be isolated from any other. Each person's future is in some way linked to all.

We can summarize this twelfth directive in three words: *goodbye, national sovereignty.* This is why the loud, aggressive hatred of Donald J Trump. The legal action in the United States to undergird this secular humanist revolutionary policy is best and most clearly seen by the current policies on illegal immigration.

We are a nation of immigrants. No one embraces immigrants as we do, and have in the past. We open our arms with love and encouragement to legal immigrants. We provide a place to live and system where they can succeed. The charge and accusation of hatred of Hispanics because we dare to desire our border controlled is a red herring. We want to protect our borders because we want to maintain our sovereignty. We don't "hate" anyone, but we want the rule of law to be upheld. We want for all people to come through an orderly process of immigration that ends in a new American citizen who is integrated into our culture. We do not demand that they shed the flavor, traditions or love of their home nation, but we believe that an orderly immigration process creates a citizen who has a fealty to the United States.

The application of a negative shroud over those who desire the laws to be enforced is focused and intentional. Journalists refer to those who use the term *illegal immigrant* as using speech that is hateful, poisonous, biased, offensive, and radical. In so describing the speech, they describe those who use it, which makes anyone who uses the term *illegal immigrant* a biased, hateful, poisonous, and radical person (see the CNN article by Charles Garcia on Friday, June 6, 2012). Terms like *bigot* and *hater* are used to describe those who wish to protect our national sovereignty and expect our elected officials to act in keeping with our Constitution to protect and defend our nation. The desire to retain our sovereignty is not in keeping with the revolutionists. The terms *illegal alien* or *illegal immigrant* are being forced out of public discourse and being replaced with the term immigrant. This is wholly inappropriate, for we are a nation of immigrants and immigrants' children and grandchildren. There is a distinction between those who have come legally and those who continue to break our borders illegally.

Defending our borders has absolutely no *aggression* in it. It is right and proper for a sovereign people to protect itself from aggressive foreign individuals who would come into the country without permission and proper paperwork. The eleventh affirmation addresses the reason behind the media, educational, and legal stand. It affirms the secular humanist vision for the world citizen.

Consider for one moment how you would defend your home against someone who wants to break in. You would use whatever means necessary to keep them out and protect your home and family. The secular humanists, through a cunning use of language, will silence any opposition to their plan to strip the country of borders.

Consider how we ought to respond to the Law of the Sea treaty, which would turn over every one of our waterways—rivers, lakes, and streams—to the control of international bodies. This treaty, proposed in 1982, has not yet been signed by the United States, though during the Obama presidency, there was a great deal of pressure brought to bear to sign it. The Senate Republicans, however, would not allow it to go forward. Should this be signed, a huge portion of our sovereignty will be lost.

These two documents, *Humanist Manifesto I* and *Humanist Manifesto II*, have a consistent unity:

1. They never move off the target for radical revolution.

2. They address all areas of life and government.

3. They establish only one common enemy to the new citizen, which is the traditional citizen who adheres to a belief in God.

4. The citizen that is their enemy not only believes in God but also believes in and desires limited government, personal freedom, and responsibility. They embrace national

sovereignty and state rights over federal directives in their daily lives with regard to laws that govern everything outside of interstate commerce and federal defense.

CHAPTER 8

These Are Crazy Extremes, Most Citizens Are in the Middle

At an early age, we are instructed that it is improper to discuss religion or politics in polite circles. Unfortunately, this little book is the intersection of both. Therein is the indiscretion, and therein is the difficultly. To open both of these personal subjects up to the light of discussion may seem foolish because there is, you will say, one point that weakens the thesis of this entire body of work. It appears as though I am discussing the *extremes* in the society, not the norm. Most people are not at the extreme of spiritual dedication, and most are not demanding an atheist environment. Most people just want to get along and live as best as they can.

As one considers the premise that secular humanists have attempted to exchange our Judeo-Christian heritage for the new spiritual base of religious secular humanism, one has to wonder whether, in fact, the institution of humanism is a result of what has already taken place in the lives of the citizens or if, as I am suggesting, there has been a systematic reprogramming of our institutions with the intent of making that exchange in our culture. In addition, we acknowledge that it appears as though the entire body of this book refers to two very distinctive, domineering religious perspectives that are warring for the hearts and minds of the American public.

Contrary to adamant, domineering religious beliefs, however, you may find in your own life that most people fall into a category somewhere in the middle. People may not consider themselves religious, may not attend any church or have ever had an affiliation with a church. They would, however, resent being categorized as atheists. I know of a group of Jews in our community that call themselves humanist Jews. They do not believe in God at all, yet they continue to refer to themselves as Jewish and to follow certain strict religious legal constraints. This is an enigma to me because I cannot fathom why one would live under any part of the Levitical law just for the sake of doing it. This group of Jewish secularists advertise and hold an annual Passover feast. They are held just for the sake of ritual and beauty, with words that are uplifting for them, but do not refer to God. The entire original Passover is a very serious remembrance of a powerful, real, and personal God, who delivers a people whom he calls "His" out of slavery. It is difficult to see the parallel from the traditional Passover to the humanist one.

Let me answer a few of the questions posed above. Most Americans are wholly unaware of the information that I am publishing here. They observe the change in social structure, but few recognize that the change is systematic and instituted according to a specific set of plans. It is undeniable that a movement toward a state-dictated establishment of the religion of atheism is moving forward and, currently, with an increasingly forceful hand of the state. What is not so well-known is that the results of the continual indoctrination of humanist ideals have not yet saturated the public mind and soul.

A YouGov survey referred by CBS on July 23, 2013, reported that 62 percent of Americans believe God created humans; 37 percent of those believed God created human beings in their present form. Only 21 percent believe that God did not play a part in human evolution, while 17 percent of those polled were not sure if God played a part in the existence of humans. YouGov also found that more people favored having creationism taught in schools than opposed it. An article by Leslie Grimard printed on July 19, 2013, reported that "a new Pew Forum poll shows that 48 percent of Americans say a decline of religion is bad for American Society." The percent of Americans that mark their religion as "none" has grown from 8 percent in 1990 to 20 percent as of May 2013. While that number of "none" has grown significantly, it is noteworthy that after many generations of atheism being taught in the public school system, enacted into law, and institutionalized through culture and entertainment, such a relatively few Americans would proclaim that there is no God. June 3, 2011, in a Gallup poll authored by Frank Newport, it was noted that more than nine out of ten Americans continue to believe in God. Despite vast changes and the intolerant stronghold in the education system, Americans respond that they do believe in God. It is notable that 1 percent of those polled had no opinion, and 8 percent said they did not believe in God. From that small glimpse of American society, we can extrapolate that there are 8 percent of the populace that are atheists, yet we have revolved all our educational system, our public gatherings, such as schools, ball games, and graduation exercises, around those 8 percent.

The theists would, no doubt, range from a general belief in a universal spirit to a life dedicated to God in whatever organized religion to which they belong. The spectrum of belief is great and has been the basis for the formation of the many and varied organized churches that are represented in America today. To mention just a few of the hundreds of doctrines that separate one group from another, some would believe in a limited atonement, some would believe that no music is to be played within the church, others believe the expression of music and statues is the very essence of spirituality, some believe that there is a specific day that must be called a Sabbath, and others believe that worship of God can take place equally well anytime and anywhere. Some would even expect formal dress for a church service, while sandals and shorts are the regular fare for others. The protection that our First Amendment affords each citizen is to worship God in the traditions that they see fit without government intrusion. It is undeniable that the bedrock of the American social structure was built upon a belief in God and specifically upon Judeo-Christian traditions. What is amazing is that *after* years of social re-engineering in schools, entertainment, and legal restraints of open acknowledgment of belief in God, the population as a whole still appears to have belief and dependence upon God.

This is precisely why it is so important to acknowledge the secular humanist system with its specific tenets. The two systems have lived side by side with few ruffled feathers because the theist community has been content to repeatedly give their ground over to a minority of atheists. In so doing, they have allowed a complete restructuring of their educational system as well as their public proclamation of fealty and dependence upon God. It is truly time that we evaluate what we have done and where we should go from here.

CHAPTER 9

Humanist Manifesto 2000

A Call for New Planetary Humanism

There is one final document that is an important body of work that cannot be ignored if we are to envision the entire plan. Earlier in this little book, I likened this plan of action to a set of architectural blueprints for a new building. The *Humanist Manifesto 2000: A Call for New Planetary Humanism* in the blueprints may be considered the "finish treatments of the structure." Up till now, we have seen the structure being built by governmental authority that is being exercised primarily in the areas of education, public expression of faith, and social law, which restructures the family, including childhood autonomy. The structure must include the fall of the United States into full humanist lockstep for the planetary humanist takeover to occur. We must have an entire economic collapse, which may remove the dollar from the international currency. Since ours is the most powerful nation on earth, and unquestionably the only one that has had the freedom of the individual tied to the belief and reliance upon the God of the Bible, with this necessity, it is again made clear why Donald J. Trump needed to be removed from office using any and all tactics available. It was imperative to remove him and to destroy both him, his family, and his movement. Judging from the executive orders that the president used during his term to secure religious freedom, one must guess that he was aware of the religious war in America.

We will not be looking at *Humanist Manifesto 2000* in any detail, because by now it is clear that our intent is to establish that there is a determined and specific blueprint to the revolution that has been instituted in our country and that the result is Two Americas growing side by side. One is supported by and fueled financially and educationally by the humanist elites; the other is the nemesis of the secular humanists and constitutes the remnants of the theist America. In the last chapter, we noted that 91 percent of Americans polled still say they believe in God. The question that is unanswered is, How many of those who believe in God would prefer that the state schools where their children are educated reflect a culturally shared belief in God?

The schism between traditional and humanist view has grown deeper and wider with each passing year. Should the revolutionaries succeed, the adherence to our original documents demands that the court system, and perhaps historians, rewrite the American story to fit the revolutionary goals. The legal structures and social mores of our founders are incompatible with the humanist principles as set forth in the documents we have just covered. Having moved through the first documents and having considered the legal and social changes that have been instituted to assert this revolutionary cycle, we can reference and overview *Humanist Manifesto 2000* and then refer you, the reader, to the book in order to give careful attention to its precepts.

Humanist Manifesto I **established the fact of the revolution that was about to begin, set forth the methods that would be used to put it into national practice, and immediately laid out the specific foundations that must be changed at all costs in order to build this new building of atheism.**

Humanist Manifesto II **built upon the foundation of atheism in the first manifesto and affirmed evolution in the public schools and institutions. It reiterated the need for actively separating church and state and, in so doing, confirmed this primary legal battle that separates our Judeo-Christian heritage from any public place or institution. This battle must be won in order to establish the new social order. It reiterates the earlier-mentioned need for one-world government, the redistribution of goods and services, which will assure equal outcomes, the autonomy of children, and the redefinition of the family unit. It demands that the free enterprise economic system, which we enjoy, be overthrown and demands that emotions and beliefs of individuals reflect humanist precepts, including, but not limited to, abortion, euthanasia, and homosexuality.**

Anyone who keeps even a limited eye on the social events and ensuing political arguments common today will easily see that the current division of Republican, Democrat, Progressive, non-Progressive, Conservative, or Liberal is ineffective and nonconstructive to the true nature of the revolution.

These terms sadly serve to keep the public frustrated because they sense a revolution is afoot but are completely unable to define its parameters or see how each new facet of the social change fits into place.

Everything is boiled down to individual political races with the tension of financial scarcity and the urgency to act to save the nation. The question remains, What are we attempting to save the nation from? Is it illegal immigration? Is it loss of individual freedom? Is it the growth and control of government in the lives of individuals? Is it loss of religious freedom? Is it the weakening of free enterprise? Or the freedom to retain gun ownership?

The answer is yes to each of these, but none of these individual battles really define what the war is about. Neither does the term *liberal* differentiate them from *conservative*. One must understand the underlying plan in order to comprehend how each of these issues works in concert to bring about a revolution in America.

There is a certain desperation that may be eliminated by ascertaining the real plan for the revolution and making a conscious decision of which worldview you, as an American citizen, desire to adopt. When considered in light of the actions instituted into public policy.

It is as though the American populace has been loaded on a train that is headed for a destination we did not select. The final destination of the policies and laws that are the outcome of instituting this worldview will be diametrically opposed to the destination our Founding Fathers planned for us. If we are to make such a final and dramatic change in our destination, we should know where we are going and *choose* to go there.

There are two other humanist documents that were written in the twentieth century that we will not cover in this book at all, *A Secular Humanist Declaration and A Declaration of Interdependence*, which will be left for the reader's own research.

Let us return to *Humanist Manifesto 2000*. This book moves us forward with breathtaking velocity out of the national perspective into the "utopian" future that awaits the world citizen. The citizen in the street screaming "Burn it down!" referring to American cities, does so with the hope in mind that it will be rebuilt into a utopian new world order!

This new volume was put out to address the vast changes in world commerce, science, technology, and the information age, believing that the religious rivalry here in the United States is moving toward the secular humanist's complete and final hold on American law and education, and the expectation that our national sovereignty is coming to a close. With this in mind, the secular humanists address fundamentalist religions worldwide that have been rekindled, contesting the principles of humanism and secularism, and that are demanding a return to the religiosity of a postmodern era.

The secular humanists believe they alone hold the key to bringing happiness to all people and solving social problems and ameliorating the human condition. They state that "there are still other dangerous tendencies in the world that are insufficiently recognized." Consider the following passage:

> We are especially concerned about anti-scientific, anti-modern trends, including the emergence of shrill fundamentalist voices and the persistence of bigotry and intolerance, whether religious, political or tribal in origin. These are the same forces in many parts of the world that oppose efforts to resolve social problems or to ameliorate the human condition:
>
> 1. The persistence of traditional spiritual attitudes which often encourage unrealistic, escapist, otherworldly approaches to social problems, inculcates disrespect for science and all to often defends archaic social institutions.
>
> 2. Many religious and political groups oppose contraception or the funding of programs designed to reduce fertility and to stabilize population growth. As a result, economic development and the reduction of poverty are hampered.
>
> 3. Many of these forces also oppose the liberation of women and wish to keep them subservient to men.
>
> 4. The world increasingly has witnessed bitter ethnic conflicts and intensified tribal rivalries. The religious dimensions to these conflicts remain largely unreported: in Yugoslavia, among Serbian Orthodox Christians and Roman Catholics, and Muslims (in Bosnia and Kosovo); in Israel and Palestine between orthodox Jews and Muslims; in Northern Ireland

between Protestants and Catholics; in Sri Lanka between Tamil Hindus and Sinhalese Buddhists; in the Punjab and Kashmir among Hindus, Muslims, and Sikhs; in East Timor between Christians and Muslims.

And the following, taken from *Humanist Manifesto* pages 20 and 21:

The *Humanist Manifesto 2000* lays out a comprehensive ethical system apart from God directed by men in a world controlled by men, dependent upon their government for provision of all basic needs in life. The exercise of this system must, by its very nature, be worldwide for control of biological and other warfare as well as other evils can be done in no other manner. The goals of providing for all equally and establishing a world with perfect eco system as well as ideal educational opportunities necessitates a tight control of all populations.

The world vision promoted in *Humanist Manifesto 2000* promises freedom, and it will require unlimited control by a small group of individuals, leaving the rest of the populace as prisoners to their direction.

Humanist Manifesto 2000 is truly a call to planetary humanism and discusses the benefits of technology in relation to ethics and reason. This manifesto is, again, set in the backdrop of no absolutes and no authority. It formulates a planetary bill of rights and responsibilities that sound as if they could be found in every schoolroom in America—Ooops! Perhaps they are found in every classroom in America. At least in the state school system.

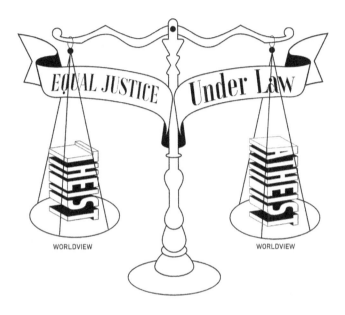

CHAPTER 10

What Do We Do Now?

As we scrutinize the specific plan for the revolution of America and take stock of how far the revolutionaries have come, it is breathtaking. The most important first step is to recognize that it is a revolution of thought, morals, economy, and politics. The revolution has been ongoing for a very long time, and there may be greater than 50 percent of the nation's population who agree with the humanist tenets and direction as described here.

The second step is to determine which direction you, as a citizen, believe we should go. In truth, there may be a majority of our citizens who are glad to turn from our founding principles. These citizens may expect that it is the government's responsibility to feed, clothe, house, and provide medical care and education for them. They may be willing and content to do a menial job for the government for these handouts or prefer to do nothing at all.

Have our citizens been so much altered in their minds and hearts as to approve of the new direction of the country? If the citizenry wishes to pursue government apart from God and embrace atheism as a national religion, let it be the citizens who stand with eyes open and embrace this revolution. However, do not let us not be led as sheep to slaughter into this established national religion of atheism and all its changes without making a conscious selection to leave our theist roots. I, for one, do not believe that our citizens would choose this road.

We citizens need to acknowledge that the many individual changes in law, morals, family life, and economics are not disjointed individual cases but rather formulate the legal fabric of an entirely new nation and, in fact, a new world order. I will reiterate one more time some battleground issues:

1. **The complete elimination of all vestiges of our Judeo-Christian heritage from schools, public places, entertainment, higher education, and professional positions.**

2. **The redefinition of marriage to eliminate Judeo-Christian ethical standards.**

3. **The redefinition of the family to include any group of individuals.**

4. **The elimination of distinctions between male and female.**

5. **The redefinition of right and wrong to eliminate absolutes in most cases.**

6. **The political establishment of gay, lesbian, and transvestite**

protected minorities to eliminate the private citizen's ability to train their children in biblical thinking regarding human sexuality.

7. The redefinition of the role of government in the lives of individuals. The government is provider of all basic needs, including food, clothing, shelter, medical care, childcare and feeding, minimum monthly income, and education.

8. Elimination of the connection of conception from human sexuality.

9. Elimination of national sovereignty.

10. Elimination of strong familial ties.

11. Silencing of all theists in both public and private settings.

12. Control of all wealth by an elite few who will have absolute power over human movement, goods, and services.

13. Absolute unquestioned authority by the elite few over all environmental issues.

14. Exacerbation of group divisions between Black and White or Hispanic and White or straight and gay. Always divide, never unite.

15. The religion of atheism is entirely *intolerant* on every level and must have complete, unquestioned rule in order for the entire plan to work.

Anytime you see an issue in the news that is accomplishing one of these goals, know that it is *not* an individual incident; it is part of a larger plan. Be assured that any court case that deals individually with freedoms regarding any of these issues is building the legal structure to complete the revolution. Nothing is being done in isolation; every single event is part of the whole.

This revolution was instituted and implemented by a relatively small group of elites coupled with a relatively small group of lawyers who have been greatly successful in part because each event is viewed by theists as just another single event and never shown in context of the overall social plan. It is time for individual citizens to count the cost of the direction we are taking. We must see public discourse begin to discuss and question the revolutionary plan so that the weight and outcome of each direction is in the open. If there are sufficient theists who remain and have a will to continue this nation with religious freedoms, I am about to pose a suggestion that could become part of our public discourse. The question may arise, Is it too late? Hope never fails! Our minds reel as we wonder, can we put on the brakes? Can we make a change? Are we entirely lost? Is there a will to go back? Is there a road back?

Since the revolutionaries have used the vehicle of the courtroom to achieve the fundamental social change, does this body of law now lock us forever into our current direction? I am not a lawyer, but I hope not.

In writing this book, I am forced to look back at how far along the revolutionary trail we have traveled. When I further consider the monumental task of having people actually see the battle we are in, it makes me shaky. I admit that it appears impossible. In the midst of the impossible, I acknowledge I serve a big God, who I believe has control of all things, and that even this has been *allowed* by Him. I have decided to fight like a warrior and hope like a giddy optimist, and I pray that you put on your rose-colored glasses and join me!

Regardless of the power of the media, the money of the politicians, the determination or organization of the revolutionaries, and the apathy of the general public, it may be true that the power of the vote still remains in the hand of the individual citizen.

This small volume will come into the public's hands just following a historic election in America where voter fraud was alleged. In addition to unverified voters, a failure to verify voter signatures on mail-in ballots and voter machines, which were allegedly controlled through sources in Italy, Germany and China who were watching and altering the vote in real-time, are just a brief summary of the alleged grievances. We do not yet have full evidence in the hands of the public regarding the truth of these allegations.

The reaction to these allegations, however, seem to add weight to their truth. Following the massive gathering of evidence, affidavits of individual citizens, and evidence regarding the dominion software, the elite reaction was to entirely silence anyone questioning the validity of the vote, block the evidence from being laid out in a court as a legal matter, and disallow the votes to be forensically examined.

In other words, there was an impenetrable wall erected around the alleged evidence so that nothing could be brought before the public. *If* the 2020 presidential election was stolen—and we do not yet have conclusive evidence one way or another—this will be the last election in American history. If the elite powers were able to effectively eliminate the citizen's vote in 2020, they will never again be allowed to have an influence. The candidates will be selected and elected by the elite few in order to bring the United States to its knees and deliver it once and forever to the one world state.

Because the results of this election have such far-reaching effects, the battle has been like none other that I have observed as an adult citizen.

I have attempted to define the "Two Americas." I can only pray that the citizens retain the right to choose our direction with their vote.

Should the final pieces of this revolution be put into place, it should be done not by the revolutionaries but by informed citizens who have seen the plan and wish to exchange their freedoms for an atheist state headed by a small group of elite politicians.

There are specific steps we must take as a nation to chart our course ahead.

1. Acknowledge both the fact of the revolution and its stated goals in *Humanist Manifesto I* and *II*. Understand that this revolution has been in action for many years.

2. Know the plan. Be able to recognize the pillars that support the revolution and are being used in education and the court systems. Have a working memory of the manifestos, for they identify the areas where legal challenge and social change will be found. Be ready to articulate each of the areas and be bold in your willingness to reveal the goals to the desire to bring about a revolution in America and to create an atheist governmental and social system. Get this concept of Two Americas and two worldviews into public discourse. Here is an easy-to-remember list that may be taken out of the book or copied.

The Revolutionary's Blueprint Shortlist

a. The secular humanists promote institutionalizing atheism, which includes the removal of God from the culture and the education system. They desire to discourage belief in God and public and private expressions of faith.

b. They consider belief in a prayer-hearing God as dangerous.

c. They desire the removal of both the written presence and the values expressed in the Ten Commandments.

d. They desire to redefine the core family away from the biblical pattern of a mother and father who care for and raise children.

e. They desire to institutionalize evolution.

f. They desire to remove students who openly believe in creation by design from access to any science degrees and eliminate those who do not share the firm belief in evolution, and thus atheism, from practicing medicine.

g. The secular humanist revolutionaries utilize environmental activism to control public dollars, curtail personal freedoms, and reorganize society.

h. Humanists promote abortion and sexual autonomy in children as early as possible.

i. Humanists promote one-world government and world courts; they work to eliminate our national sovereignty.

j. Secular humanists have designed a new economic system for our nation. Free enterprise will be replaced with Socialism and redistribution of goods and wealth globally.

k. Humanists would transfer dependence on the individual and God for personal needs to dependence on the governmental system that will distribute minimum services of food, clothing, housing and medicine, education, and childcare equally among all peoples.

l. Humanists desire to have control of children as early and as fully as possible. Their design is that children look to the state with dependence for their visible needs, such as food, education, and health care.

m. Secular humanists will institute government programs that support dependence on government and subsistence living. They will utilize tax structure and government programs to promote single-parent households. These parents tend to be more greatly fearful, less independent, and more likely to look to government rather than God or a spouse for their support.

n. The humanists promote situational ethics and moral autonomy throughout the state school education.

o. Humanists institute programs where children learn to depend on government and others rather than God, their parents, or their core family.

How Would Citizens Desiring to Restore Our founding Principles Go About It?

It is important that we take seriously the change agents that the revolutionaries have used and are using. The state school system, the media and entertainment, and the courts have been entirely co-opted for their message, and in fact, they are used to exercise an intolerant demand to embrace atheist secular humanism.

If we desire to hear from both of the two groups in America and to allow those groups to set the direction for our national future, we will need to determine by what way the citizenry can express their fealty for one system over another. We will not know which direction the nation is going until we pose the question to the populace in a way that they have a means to express their own beliefs. This is a historic moment, and **we must agree to hear one another, and we must agree that citizens from each worldview should have the freedom to pursue the happiness promised in our Declaration.**

I will assume that we will not turn the media in a direction to honor theists anytime soon. The media, however, represents a free market. As citizens begin to discuss the Two Americas not in the light of race or wealth but in the light of theism and atheism, it is not impossible to consider that some media outlets will emerge who will more nearly identify with theists, and some who will more nearly identify with atheists. We must agree that we can disagree.

Any change in the court system will be a very slow process of new political leadership and then new appointments. This could literally take decades.

The greatest impact that secular humanists have had is the takeover of the public school system. This access granted them an opportunity to indoctrinate large numbers of children to a worldview of atheism every day, year after year. Even if a child comes from a home that reflects a belief in God, the slow stripping away of their beliefs and replacement with the state authoritative indoctrination, followed by the silencing of parents and other children, has successfully separated many children from their parents' worldviews and moral perspectives.

1. The first thing individual citizens must do is to define the two world systems that are at odds with one another.

2. Get off the fence and "pick a team," so to speak. Those who decide that a theist worldview fits their perspective may not be actively involved with a church at all. They may have no denominational affiliation; they may have had a brief Sunday school class forty years ago that has left a strong sense of belief that there is a god who rules the universe. Some will see Him as a personal God to whom they pray, while others will see God as an unknown quantity who set the world a-spinning and has stepped back out of reach, but they have a reverence and belief that when all is said and done, "there is a god and they are not him."

There are those who will read *Humanist Manifesto I* and *II* and breathe a sigh of relief for it will say to them that everything they have longed for would come true but they did not know there was a formulated plan. They are unabashedly atheists. They would be satisfied to destroy our original documents and move on.

I suggest we do two things immediately, like, right now, like, today, if possible!

Develop a litmus test for the citizenry based on the two worldviews. This litmus test would be given to every candidate for every office. Make the test very succinct.

1. Theists would embrace the traditional constitutional worldview.

2. Atheists would embrace the view of the revolutionary.

3. Each and every candidate for any American office must take and publish openly the results of the test. This would include those who run for dogcatcher and school board to the president of the United States. In this way any citizen who votes will not be surprised by the worldview that will be reflected by the candidate once they are an officeholder. This would, in no way, establish religion as a test for office but define a candidate's worldview.

Institute this questionnaire as a means of ascertaining worldview. There are tests of background, capabilities, and management skills that should be a part of selecting a candidate—but worldview will ultimately be the guiding force behind any man's or woman's passions, their lawmaking direction, and the direction that will be taken in their public spending allocations.

To make certain their answers are succinct, I suggest that they just check off their preferences, not comment on them. The answers to such a questionnaire as I am suggesting below will give citizens a very clear and immediate understanding of a candidate's worldview and allegiance. Most people are no longer divided in their views. They are either a humanist revolutionary or a traditionalist. We must lessen the impact of such terms as *Liberal, Conservative, Progressive, Republican, Libertarian*, and *Democrat*. These terms are ultimately confusing and do not inform a voter of the worldview that the candidate will attempt to substantiate during their time as an elected official.

Party affiliation is far less important than the understanding of the exact direction that the representatives desire to take the nation. The test should be as follows:

1. Which view of the world do you, as a candidate, support?

   a. A traditional system that acknowledges a sovereign God as our Redeemer and Maker and personally knowable.
   b. An atheist who believes that we are our own final arbiter.

2. Do you believe the government should supply a basic cost-of-living salary to all citizens?

   a. Yes.
   b. No.

3. Would you choose judges that would protect all life?

   a. Yes.
   b. No.

4. Do you believe the United States should strive to retain her national sovereignty?

   a. Yes.
   b. No.

5. Should funding be provided for abortion services?

   a. Yes.
   b. No.

6. Circle one of the following:

   a. Personal responsibility for all citizens to provide for the food, clothing, housing, education, medical care, and child-rearing for yourself and your family.

b. Government responsibility to provide food, clothing, housing, minimum basic wage, and medical care for citizens.

a. Government's responsibility is to provide a structure that allows individuals to succeed according to their intelligence, work ethic, and individual abilities.
b. Government's responsibility is to ensure equal outcomes for all people to fail or succeed.

a. Dependence on God and self.
b. Dependence upon the government.

a. Government to provide national defense and infrastructure of roads and highways through the taxes collected from its citizens.
b. Government to limit our defense capabilities to ensure defense equity for all nations.

a. Free enterprise economic system.
b. Socialism as a national economic system.

a. Encourage all independent businesses
b. Institutionalize and control industry under the hand of government through permitting EPA and other means.

a. The people grant to government limited rights to rule. The citizens' rights to freedom are given by God and hence cannot be taken away.
b. The government grants limited freedom to citizens, which can be changed at its will.

7. The people must knowingly do which of the following:

a. Relinquish their rights to government by their own consent. Relinquish them.
b. The government may assert power as they see fit to

accomplish their longterm goals for the society. (Do you believe a governor should exercise his authority to limit the size of soda a citizen can purchase?)

a. Retain the first two paragraphs as written in the Declaration of Independence.
b. Adopt a rewrite of the first two paragraphs of the Declaration of Independence to eliminate the references to God and Creator and state that the government is granted the job of determining what will make people happy and safe and provide those things according to its desires. That the people agree to submit themselves to the powerful hand of the government and to exchange all freedom for the promise of such safety and provision as the benevolent governing authorities are desiring to bestow.

a. Institute immediate education reform to allow parents to select a public school that supports their worldview.
b. Continue to push for the current one-worldview system.

Each candidate should be required to provide to the voting public a questionnaire similar to the one above. This type of questionnaire would be crucial for the citizen to be assured which direction this public servant plans to take the citizens.

Should the citizens decide to relinquish their rights and exchange the dependence on God for dependence on government, it will be a clear historic choice. We "frogs" will have gotten out of the proverbial pot and made a decision as to where our future and our children's future will lie.

The election of individual representatives will begin to turn the nation as a whole in one known direction or another. The revolution will be brought into the light of day.

Additionally, as long as we remain under the current Declaration and the Constitution, the changes that follow must be immediately instituted.

We must acknowledge that we have diametrically opposing systems growing alongside one another in the United States.

Education Is the Most Important Key

We must acknowledge that the public education system should not be developed exclusively around one worldview. The United States public education system must be sufficiently tolerant to provide public education paid for by tax dollars that is suitable to parents. Two systems should be offered, and parents should have the right to sign their children into the schools that most nearly reflect their family worldview.

I have two separate suggestions, either of which could be quickly and easily instituted with a new federal law. The law could be simple and is stated below:

> We recognize that education should be provided to reflect the worldview of the individual families in the communities. We acknowledge that the worldview expressed in our Declaration of Independence, and other historic documents, specifically acknowledges and gives reverence to God, as expressed in the Bible. We further acknowledge that as we receive our rights directly from Him, we, the citizens, may grant a body politic certain limited powers to govern. We believe that this worldview includes the Ten Commandments as a part of our acceptable historical-moral framework.

The second worldview, which is currently available in all public school systems, is education without the mention of a Creator, with no absolute moral framework that could be noted from the Bible or any other religious text. While this system appears to be a system where God is absent, in fact, it is a system where the education of our children takes place as though there is no God, which reflects the belief system of atheism.

Whereas the citizens no longer find a single-worldview education system acceptable.

Whereas parents should have a right to choose the educational system that they prefer for their children and one that is in keeping with their own worldview.

And whereas monies are received from citizens in order to support a public education system. We agree to the following.

Federal funding for education to individual school districts would be contingent upon the availability of both a traditional theist school program and a humanist program. The parents may direct their child to a system that most closely suits their worldview. Each school district will provide both systems in proportion to the number of students enrolled. It will be agreed that this does not constitute the establishment of a religion but rather the availability of a worldview that either acknowledges God and sets the curriculum accordingly or does not acknowledge God and sets their curriculum accordingly. The two systems would allow for parents to have their children taught within a framework that is supportive of their family views and values. The educational systems would be defined as follows.

One system would be based on traditional American values, as stated in the Declaration of Independence. The parents would accept something similar to the following statement in order to register their child:

1. This educational institution acknowledges the existence of God as Creator. We will celebrate the traditional Christian holidays of Christmas and Easter with the reverence, music, and traditional events that those holidays have enjoyed in the past history of United States children. We will celebrate Hanukkah and other appropriate traditions that acknowledge God.

2. We will have the freedom to display and read the Ten Commandments. Individual boards of education may decide whether the Ten Commandments are to be used as a tool to teach the moral and civic qualities listed in these commandments.

3. Prayer will be allowed.

4. Teaching of creation as a viable scientific method of explaining our beginnings will be allowed. Materials may be drawn from the vast resources on both creation and evolution.

5. Sex education will be taught within the framework of moral responsibility and the traditional family structure.

6. Free enterprise and Capitalism will be taught.

7. The sovereignty of the United States will be upheld, and the political practices that support our sovereignty will be an expected part of the curriculum.

8. Literature will be selected, with the specific intent of teaching the moral values of humility, thrift, selflessness, kindness, courage, fidelity, trust, love of family, love of country, and love of God.

9. While God will be honored and acknowledged in all ways, no specific doctrines will be taught to give preference of a specific religious sect, thus fulfilling the true intent of the establishment of the religion clause.

One system would be based on secular humanism, as designed and dictated from the *Humanist Manifestos*. The parents would accept something similar to the following statement in order to choose the system:

1. This educational institution is rooted and grounded in the firm belief that there is no God and that man is the final arbiter of the earth and its social systems.

2. There will be no mention of God in holiday, song, and literature or classroom discussion, except for the specific study of mythology, in which we may discuss the mythical belief in

God or gods.

3. Prayer of any kind will not be allowed, nor will the exhibition of either jewelry or artwork displaying any traditionally religious symbols or pictures.

4. Science will be firmly rooted in evolution and only evolution for the explanation of our planetary beginnings.

5. The instruction in caring for the planet and our responsibility to keep planet Earth alive and livable will be a primary focus of our education.

6. The Planetary Bill of Rights, as posed in the *Humanist Manifesto*, will be a part of the curricula appropriately taught at each grade level.

7. The International Children's Bill of Rights will be taught.

8. Music, art, and literature will be taught, with a focus on unifying the planet under one governmental system.

9. The students will be taught economics from the perspective of a collective, where government takes from some to give to others in order that all people will have a uniform standard of living provided by government.

This basic selection for world systems will be offered at the elementary, junior high, and high school systems and will also be available at the federally supported university-level schools. In the event that there are only two universities in a given state that are state funded, one will supply education from the theistic worldview, and one from the atheistic worldview. General enrollment in each will dictate future resource allocation.

School districts would have twelve months to fully implement the school choice as soon as the Freedom of Worldview in Education Act could be passed.

The second suggestion is similar to the first in that it provides complete, autonomous choice for the parents. This choice would constitute an abandonment of public school funding as we know it, with a period of three years to phase into full-implementation vouchers for parents to select their child's education. The community schools would be given freedom for atheisticor theistic-based school systems. They would have three years to engage their own community, which would, in a real sense, become their "customers" of education. The schools would put together an educational system that would be attractive and fulfilling to the greatest number of students.

This education system that would allow for communities to vote with their voucher dollars for the systems that they believe would best provide an excellent education reflective of their personal home values and their hopes and dreams for their children.

The schools that receive voucher monies must fulfill certain requirements:

- Demonstrate a safe environment in which children can learn.

- Demonstrate a fully formed curriculum that could obtain accreditation within two years.
- Demonstrate the administrative organization that would enhance learning.

- Be financially audited no less than one time every three years.

- Have fines for those people who defraud children either by taking their money without educating them or by failing to handle the finances obtained through the vouchers in an improper way.

If the populace as a majority desires to retain the right to the covenant form of government described in the Declaration of Independence, we need to elect senators and congressmen who want to uphold the first paragraph of our Declaration and retain the covenant government established by our forefathers. If, however, the majority of the citizenry is fully convinced that it is time for a revolutionary change, let us rewrite our documents to fit the reality of the nation.

Government Action

The elected officials must acknowledge the blueprint of the revolutionaries, which has moved us to this new place, where, as the writers of the manifesto declared, we have entered the twenty-first century and the time of the humanist.

Having acknowledged the move away from the Creator, we must certainly now either reaffirm our roots and allow God back into our public institutions or move on fully, eyes open, to new documents describing the new character and nature of the government that will guide us into the future.

The time for a showdown between worldviews is here, and we must be fully informed. The population as a whole must understand the two opposing sides and where each of the national philosophies will take us. There can be no clearer way than to read the manifestos, observe how they have been enacted, and then look at the lists provided for the differences in the schools, which we have just read.

Should the populace decide to retain our current form of government, there should be a reinstitution of the Ten Commandments as a commonly adopted and agreed-upon moral foundation. These are reverenced by Jews, Christians, Jehovah's Witnesses, Mormons, Congregationalists, Evangelicals, Catholics, Presbyterians, SeventhDay Adventists, Wesleyans, etc., but just because many individual religious institutions are likeminded upon certain commonly held documents, this should not be misconstrued as the establishment of a national religion. Each of these sects is distinct and different. Each has distinctions of doctrine that separate them from another. Their similarities are what they all have in common with our Declaration of Independence and all our founding documents—they hold a belief in a Creator God, as expressed in the Bible.

Thus, in welcoming the Ten Commandments back to the public arena, we will simply be re-embracing a very succinct and small group of shared moral values back to our nation, with no purpose of establishing a religion.

We need to be clear and unflinching about the bullying that has been done in public, in private, and in the courts to unabashedly point a finger of intolerance at those who place their hope and faith in God. Each has a right to their own perspective; no specific religious doctrine will be given any fuller acclaim than any other, but the 90 percent of the nation must not be hushed by intolerance, and our children must not be cudgeled into public state schools set on indoctrination rather than instruction.

Christmas and Hanukkah are part of the cultural glue that holds us together and brings us to a point of shared memories, values, and events. Both celebrations are in keeping with our declared values. They should be allowed full access to the public arena and allowed to be openly celebrated. The intolerance of atheism as a state religion should not silence those who acknowledge a Creator. Those who do not wish to take part in these holidays have full freedom to refrain from such holiday celebrations.

If, however, we complete the revolution and institute atheism as our state religion, we should do away with all government paid leave for any holidays, including Easter and Christmas. We should eliminate the excess financial burden, the decorations, the sales, and the cultural acknowledgment of these holidays and allow those who still retain them to do so in their homes.

Economy

If we retain our current system, we should enjoy and celebrate our free market economy. The economy will be open to all that come and will shun redistribution of money.

We recognize that we are a generous and compassionate people and wealth is not a prerequisite to happiness. The Declaration allows free will to pursue happiness, in contrast with humanism, which guarantees that the government will provide happiness. We will allow the individual to define their happiness and determine how they shall obtain it—that is, if we remain under our current system.

We will limit our government to a size and scope that allows for the individual workman to keep the money earned, with a limited portion going to the government, which has as its duties those as so enumerated by the populace, and nothing more.

Sovereignty

If we choose to remain under our current system, we will begin to fight to regain and retain our national sovereignty. Just as the *Humanist Manifesto* includes many things that must be done, we *must* now mention things that must be done so that we can keep this precious republic.

1. No treaties granting world courts control in our land. We can protect our borders and demand that immigrants honor our borders and our sovereignty.

2. Rigorously set about to identify every illegal alien in our nation. They must have a specific path given to citizenship, but the cost of their illegal entry is to forfeit the right to vote. Their children may vote as citizens, but those who have broken our laws to enter must pay the high price of the loss of their vote. This limitation is reasonable and not punitive. This limited right to citizenship is only for the individual who broke our laws; once

they have completed the naturalization process, their children, if they live here in the United States, will be considered full citizens.

3. No family members will be allowed to be imported to join the citizen once they complete the naturalization process. They must choose between America and citizenship or their native land with their family members. The naturalization process will coincide with what we currently use, which includes the ability to read, speak, and write English. Hence, the burden and cost of printing ballots in numerous languages will be unnecessary and terminated. All ballots will be produced in English.

4. Those noncitizens who are charged and convicted of the commission of a crime in the United States must agree to a prominent tattoo identifying them as having been charged with a crime by the United States. Since they have broken into our country illegally, they will be returned to their own country so that we will not have the expense of housing them in the future. Their individual countries will determine how to deliver a punishment for a crime they are convicted of in the United States.

5. Whatever sentence they receive from a United States court will be automatically and immediately doubled should they be caught in the United States again.

6. Their arrest and deportation will require that they sign a statement that will be kept on file in the ICE office, as well as at the state level in the state where the crime was committed and the person was found guilty. This is designed as a formidable deterrent to illegal re-entry into the United States.

7. This signed statement will state that should they ever be found in the United States again, they waive the right of a trial and will accept the full extent of the law for the crime they were

accused of.

8. This will save the legal system the burden for the costs of trial and conviction. This will also serve as a disincentive to return to America illegally. It will have the effect of stopping repeated offenses of illegal immigrants, protecting our citizenry, and providing an expedited means of handling these criminals.

It may be that some will say that this little book is simplistic! But for every person who has wondered what has happened to our once-amazing nation, look no further.

It may be that both worldviews having been outlined, there would be those who, while believing in God, have put their trust in government. So be it. There may be those who don't have a deep commitment to God but know that government does not provide the answer. So be it again! We need to see how neatly all the social change fits together, and finally, we need to choose a direction.

I would invite you to delve into some additional suggested readings below.

Suggested Reading

I am placing these reading materials into two categories. One is a category of books by authors regarding intelligent design; the other is a category of books that directly deal with the topic of this book, *The Second Revolution: From Theism to Atheism*. I am also placing these books somewhat in "order," or suggested order of reading. Obviously, if you become very interested in this topic, some of these books may spark your interest more readily than others; however, reading the books in the order given will build a significant understanding of the process that has taken place.

1. *Humanist Manifesto 2000*, drafted by Paul Kurtz

2. *Forbidden Fruit*, by Paul Kurtz

3. *The Closing of the American Mind*, by Allan Bloom

4. *The Religion of Secular Humanism in the Public Schools*, by Homer Duncan

5. *The Founder's Key*, by Larry P. Arnn

6. *7 Men Who Rule the World from the Grave*, by Dave Breese

7. *The Third Reich in Power*, by Richard J. Evans

8. *The Rise and Fall of the Third Reich*, by William Shirer

9. *Tomorrow Will Be Better: An Autobiography Written by Someone Who Lived through the Nazi Takeover*, by Zdena Kapral

10. *A Christian Worldview* (five-volume set), by Francis A. Schaeffer

11. *The Professors: The 101 Most Dangerous Academics in America*, by David Horowitz

12. *The Road to Serfdom*, by Friedrich A. Hayek

13. *Liberty and Tyranny*, by Mark R. Levin

14. *Understanding the Times*, by David A. Noebel

15. *Godless: The Church of Liberalism*, by Ann Coulter

16. *Lives of the Signers of the Declaration of Independence*, reprinted from an 1848 original, available through WallBuilders

17. *The Death of the West*, by Patrick J. Buchanan

Design Material

1. *More Than Meets the Eye*, by Richard Swenson, MD (a must-read)

2. *Unlocking the Mystery of Life* DVD, by Michael J. Behe

3. *Darwin's Black Box*, by Michael J. Behe

4. *The Edge of Evolution*, by Michael J. Behe

5. *Signature in the Cell*, by Stephen Meyer (a must-read)

6. *The Hidden Face of God*, by Gerald L. Schroeder

7. *Science and Evidence for Design in the Universe*, by Stephen Meyer and Michael J. Behe

8. *The Design Revolution: Answering the Toughest Questions about Intelligent Design*, by William A. Dembski (another must-read)

9. *The Modern Creation* trilogy, by Henry M. Morris and John D. Morris

10. *The Long War Against God*, by Henry M. Morris

The Children's Bill of Rights

(April 20, 1996)

We, Children from seven countries and three continents, having communicated with each other over the Internet, agree that the following are natural rights of Children all over the world, and hereby ratify them:

Preamble

We believe that a successful society invests its best resources and hopes in the success of its children. An unsuccessful society ignores or maltreats its children.

Children are the future of our species. How a society treats its children is a direct reflection of how that society looks at its future. The Children's Bill of Rights proposes rights for children that all adults on Earth should honor, so that we may help create the very best future for ourselves and, in turn, our own children.

A moral and competent society is one that respects and upholds the rights of its children. A society that fails to do so is immoral and incompetent.

Articles of the Children's Bill of Rights

Section I: Articles that are implemented immediately

1. Children's universal rights

   As compared to adults, children until the age of 18 have the right to receive special care and protection.

   Children all have the same rights, no matter what country they were born in or are living in, what their sex is, what their race is, or what their religion is.

2. Right to inherit a better world

   Children have the right to inherit a world that is at least as good as the one their parents inherited.

   Children have a responsibility to think about how they will leave a better world to their children, and, when they become adults, they have the right and duty to act on this.

3. Right to influence the future

   Children have the right to participate in discussions having to do with the directions our society is taking—on the large political, economic, social, and educational issues and policies—so that children can help create the kind of world they will grow up in.

Adults have an obligation to communicate their views of these large issues in terms that children can understand, and provide children with the same information that is available to all adults.

Children have the right to understand how things change within society, and to learn how to influence these changes.

4. Right to freedom of thought, opinion, expression, conscience, and religion

Every child has the right to express his or her opinion freely, and adults should address that opinion with the child in every decision that affects him or her. Children have the right to carry out research to help form these opinions.

Children have the right to express their views, obtain information, and make ideas or information known.

Children have the right to form their own views in matters of conscience and religion.

5. Right to media access

Children have guaranteed access to all important communications media so that they may communicate nationally and internationally amongst themselves and with adults.

6. Right to participate in decisions affecting children
Children have the right to participate in all committees and decisions that make plans and set policies that directly or indirectly affect children.

7. Right to privacy

Children have the right to privacy to the same extent adults have.

8. Right to respect and courtesy

Children should be treated with respect and courtesy by adults, as well as by other children.

9. Right to an identity

Children separated from their birth parents at birth or at an early age have the right to know that this happened. Children have the right to know their name, who their birth parents are, and when and where they were born.

10. Right to freedom of association

Children have the right to meet with others, and to join or form associations, equivalent to that held by adults.

11. Right to care and nurturing

Children have the right to have nurturing and caring parents or guardians.

12. Right to leisure and play

Children have the right to leisure, play, and participation in cultural and artistic activities. Children have the right to a enjoy at least a few hours every day when they are free from worries.

13. Right to safe work

Children have the right to be protected from work that threatens their health, education, or development.

Children have the right to have pocket money so that they may learn to manage money.

14. Right to an adequate standard of living

Every child has the right to a standard of living adequate for his or her physical, mental, spiritual, moral, and social development, no matter how wealthy his or her parents are.

15. Right to life, physical integrity and protection from maltreatment

Children have the right to be protected from all forms of maltreatment by any adult, including a parent. This includes but is not limited to: physical abuse, including torture, violence, hitting and slapping; harmful drugs, including alcohol and tobacco; mental abuse; and sexual abuse. Infanticide is prohibited. No child shall be forced into marriage.

16 Right to a diverse environment and creativity

Children have the right to have many different things, people, and ideas in their environment.

Children have the right to listen to music of their choice. Children have the right NOT to have their creativity stifled.

17. Right to education

Every child has the right to education, education that aims to develop his or her personality, talents, and mental and physical abilities to the fullest extent, no matter how wealthy the child's parents are.

Education should foster respect for a child's parents, for the child's own cultural identity, language and values, as well as for the cultural background and values of others.

Children have the right to an excellent education in any school. Schools will differ not in the quality of the education they offer, but only in their philosophies of teaching, and what professional specializations they stress.

18. Right to access appropriate information and to a balanced depiction

Of reality Adults have the obligation to provide children with information from several different sources.

Children should be protected from materials adults consider harmful.

Children have the right to have reality presented to them in a balanced and accurately representative fashion.

19. Right not to be exposed to prejudice

Children have the right NOT to be taught that one group (racial, national, religious, etc.) is superior to another.

Section II: Articles that require social or national policies

1. The right to a clean environment

Children have a right to a clean environment (water, air, ground, sea).

2. Right to a small national debt

Governments and countries must decrease national debt which will have to be paid for by future generations.

3. Right to vote

Children over 14 have the right to vote on issues that directly affect children, in all local, regional, national and international elections.

4. Right to medical care

Children have the right to be kept alive and in the best health and medical care science can provide, no matter how wealthy their parents are.

5. Legal rights

Children accused of crimes have at least the same legal rights as adults.

No child shall be institutionalized against her or his will without due process rights.

6. Right not to participate in war

Young people under 21 have the right NOT to go to war.

The Children's Bill of Rights Background

In 1996, several hundred children from around the world drafted The Children's Bill of Rights. The Bill lists the rights that all Children have so that they can grow up free from abuse, thrive in the world, and participate in influencing the shape of their future.

Children's Rights

Prevention of child abuse is original focus.

Over the past several years, we have become increasingly aware of the difficulty the world is having ensuring that children are brought up in a way that enables them to thrive. Initially, such concerns focused on obvious forms of child abuse: wars that targeted non-combatants and children, inter-ethnic genocide, child malnutrition, diseased environments, and social and even parental abuse. Efforts were made by some countries, the United Nations, and a plethora of private philanthropic organizations to tackle these abuses, and the first pioneering notions of children's rights emerged. But the children, themselves, had yet to be heard from.

As our understanding of these issues deepened, the concerns went beyond abuse to address more systemic, inter-generational problems. Not only did people become increasingly concerned with whether kids would be able to flourish in today's world, but whether they would be able to flourish to tomorrow's world, a world that will differ in fundamental ways from today's, yet in ways that today we don't still fully understand.

Children's rights take on a larger perspective.

In 1995, an effort was launched to address children's rights and their roles in society from this larger perspective, and to do it through the ideas, needs, and voices of kids themselves. This effort is called The Kids' Campaign. The first project was to design a Children's Bill of Rights. This was accomplished in the Spring of 1996 through the extraordinary medium of the Kidlink, an Internet organization that brings together hundreds of school children around the world and provides them with a "space" in which to express themselves and share their ideas through a wide variety of projects.

The Children's Bill of Rights

The Children's Bill of Rights was drafted and ratified by over 650 children from seven countries. The Rights range from the traditional abuse-prevention ones, to those that will ensure kids the ability to influence the shape of their own future. The Children's Bill of Rights does not ask adults or governments to ratify the Bill before it takes effect. It is adopted by the children themselves, and serves as the basis for their demand that adults treat them as partners in the processes of human progress.

Children, adults and organizations are invited to support the Children's Bill of Rights, and may list your support formally, if you wish, with the CBOR Secretariat.

The CBOR Secretariat

A Children's Bill of Rights (CBOR) Secretariat has been established to coordinate activities surrounding the CBOR, including its broad dissemination and the formation of strategic alliances with other children's organizations.

The secretariat may be contacted by postal mail at 5504 Scioto Road Bethesda, Maryland, 20816.

Linda is a wife, mother, grandmother, educator, active citizen, and successful businesswoman! She graduated university in 1975 with a BA in English literature and teaching certificate. Soon after graduation, she had an awakening which precipitated a turn from feminist to active prolife advocate. Her advocacy led to debates with the local Planned Parenthood president and a lead in introducing pro-Family Life education in the public schools. In 1977, she attended a series of lectures introducing her to the *Humanist Manifestos*. This was her "second awakening." She was now out of the dark and into the full sunshine. She could recognize the roots of our education system and has now watched the effects of the *Humanist Manifesto* principles implemented in schools, culture, law, public policy, and media. In the same way, Saul Alinsky instructs this generation with how to disrupt the nation. The *Humanist Manifesto* is the blueprint to change the citizen. This information is the passion of her life, and she now addresses it in the blueprint for Two Americas.

Visit www.2americas.net for more information.

CPSIA information can be obtained
at www.ICGtesting.com
Printed in the USA
FSHW012030210721